D0876244

THIS BOOK
BELONGS TO

_____
_____

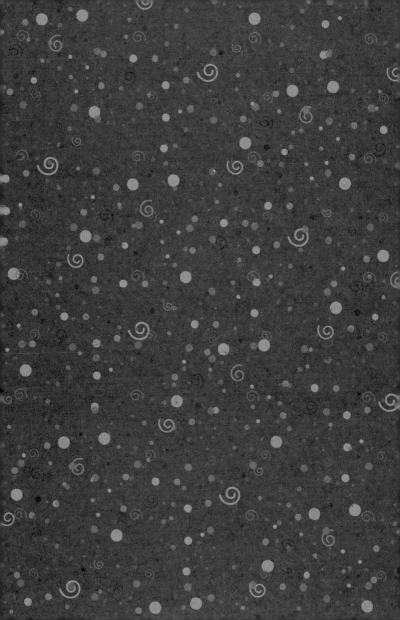

A
LITTLE
GOD
TIME

FOR
GRADUATES

BroadStreet
P U B L I S H I N G

BroadStreet Publishing Group, LLC
Racine, Wisconsin, USA
BroadStreetPublishing.com

A LITTLE GOD TIME FOR GRADUATES

FOR THE LORD GOD
IS OUR SUN AND OUR SHIELD.
HE GIVES US GRACE AND GLORY.
THE LORD WILL WITHHOLD NO
GOOD THING FROM THOSE
WHO DO WHAT IS RIGHT.

PSALM 84:11 NLT

INTRODUCTION

This devotional is written just for
graduates—like you! It will engage
you in topics specific to what you face
each day. Read about themes like
purpose, courage, identity, faithfulness,
and hope, and be encouraged to find
everything you need in Christ.

Gain confidence as you learn that
the God who created you has a plan
for your life. As you embrace his words
of truth, be filled with joy, strength,
wisdom, and renewed purpose for the
day ahead.

JANUARY

Before he made the world, God chose
us to be his very own through what
Christ would do for us; he decided
then to make us holy in his eyes,
without a single fault—we who stand
before him covered with his love.

EPHESIANS 1:4 TLB

STARTING NEW

It was you who formed my inward parts;
you knit me together in my mother's womb.
I praise you, for I am fearfully and wonderfully made.
Wonderful are your works; that I know very well.

PSALM 139:13-14 NRSV

Whenever you embark on something new, it is important to have an open mind. Starting new isn't easy. You have to decide what you are willing to give up or put up with. Resetting your life might mean leaving behind an old habit, an unhealthy relationship, your friends, or your past.

Remember that God knows you. He knows your capabilities; he knows your present and future challenges; and he knows how he will cultivate your character. When you lose heart, God knows you can succeed. When you feel out of place, he knows you are there for a reason. When you feel alone, he knows the people you will meet. When you feel like giving up, he knows what you can accomplish.

God created you for this very moment in your life. You are on your way to something new.

Lord, as I begin this new chapter of my life, I am filled with great anticipation. Help me to maintain a positive attitude. Give me courage when I am weak and tenacity when life is tough. Thank you for the confidence that you know me and will help me succeed.

MILLENNIALS AND THE BIBLE

"People are like grass; their beauty is like a flower in the field. The grass withers and the flower fades. But the word of the Lord remains forever."
And that word is the Good News that was preached to you.
1 PETER 1:24-25 NLT

A recent study from the Barna Group discovered a uniqueness about millennials and their religious beliefs. Millennials want the real deal. They want a faith that changes people for the better, or they don't want it at all. Ninety-six percent of Christian millennials said that reading the Bible is more important to them than going to church, worship, or even prayer.

What's the big deal about the Bible? The Bible is the living Word of God. Scripture itself has power. It can directly impact your life and circumstance. God speaks to you through its pages, offering encouragement, counsel, and wisdom. When you take in his words, you are changed.

Don't believe it? Maybe you should give it a try. If you have never read the Bible, consider beginning with Proverbs. There is one chapter for every day of the month. Savor the Word, and let it seep deep into your heart. Act on what you read. Your life will be transformed as you make this best-selling book part of your daily life.

Father God, sometimes I read the Bible and come up dry. Help me to try again with fresh eyes. Help me to taste your power and experience you through your Word.

BUILT ON PURPOSE

It was you who formed my inward parts;
you knit me together in my mother's womb.
I praise you, for I am fearfully and wonderfully made.
Wonderful are your works;
that I know very well.

PSALM 139:13-14 NRSV

Even before you were born, the Lord was busy working on you. God knew what color your eyes were going to be, and how thick or thin or curly or straight your hair would turn out. And even better, he knew all the character traits that add up to exactly what makes you, you!

Here's the best thing: God doesn't make mistakes. What does that mean for you? It means that he knew what he was doing with every trait he gave you. He thinks you are wonderful! You may be questioning why you were born with such and such, or why you have this or that personality trait. But he built you that way on purpose, to use it for his glory, because he saw the beauty in it!

Lord, help me to see how wonderfully you've made me, each and every day.

SUBMISSION?

Submit therefore to God.
Resist the devil and he will flee from you.

JAMES 4:7 NASB

One of the hardest things to do in life is to submit to someone else's authority. Giving up control sounds like a terrible idea! We want complete jurisdiction over the decisions we make, right? And yet, we're asked to give that up. As believers in Christ, we are told that we need to give our lives over to him.

Submission means to yield to another person. In Christ's case, he is superior to us in every way, shape, and form. Although he is superior, and though he could have forced us all into submission, he has given us the choice. We can choose to live a better life through him, full of wisdom and joy, or we can choose otherwise. He loves us enough to let us decide.

Lord, I pray I'd choose daily to submit myself to you. Give me wisdom in my decisions and the joy that comes from knowing you in a deep and real way. Thank you for giving me the choice, and for loving me so well.

WHO'S GOT YOUR BACK?

What shall we say about such wonderful things as these?
If God is for us, who can ever be against us?

ROMANS 8:31 NLT

It's really hard when people pass rumors that are unkind or untrue. Sometimes, people may be against you because you follow Jesus. It can feel like you will be the loser in this war.

Remember, the battle is not yours but the Lord's! You do not need to argue, plead, reason, or defend yourself. God will be your defender, and your best offense is to be still. When you hold back from sharing your side of the story, the Lord can work on your behalf.

God's got your back. You will not be destroyed. All you have to do is stand on the Word, on wise advice, and on the Lord's solid presence in your life. When the battle subsides, you will be stronger, kinder, and wiser.

Lord, this battle I am facing is hard. Help me trust you as my defender rather than plan my own attack. I pray that someone will have my back, and let me stand strong while I wait.

KNOCKED TO YOUR KNEES

Submit therefore to God.
Resist the devil and he will flee from you.

JAMES 4:7 NASB

One of devil's biggest victories is getting people to believe that he doesn't exist. But he's not hard to recognize. When your life is in turmoil, he's never far away.

The devil preys on your weaknesses, and he wants you to be miserable. If he can't knock you to your knees in one area, he knows exactly where to go after you next. He works overtime to destroy your relationships and everything that matters to you, and that's no joke.

Hard work and clever conversations will not fix your problems. The devil will outwit you. There are two ways to get this guy to leave the building. First, obey God. Living in God's will is the safest place to be. Being in the wrong place, with the wrong people, and doing the wrong things will lead you down the enemy's path to destruction. Submitting to the Lord will bring good things into your life. Second, pray. When you get knocked to your knees, stay there and pray. Why not start your day there? Prayer sends the devil packing.

Jesus, send the devil where he belongs. Please remove his presence from my life and this situation. Help me to avoid temptation and to call on you in prayer. Thank you for my freedom in you.

BRUSH IT OFF

Whoever loves discipline loves knowledge,
but whoever hates correction is stupid.

PROVERBS 12:1 NIV

How do you handle correction? Do you make excuses? Blame someone else? Lose confidence? Or do you take responsibility? Does it discourage you, or does it inspire you to do better?

Whether it is in your job, your faith walk, a relationship, school, weight loss, or athletics, having the ability to accept a failure or criticism and then brush it off is critical to your growth. Baseball players are pretty good at brushing off disappointment. When they slide into second and the ump calls them out, they hop up and brush off their pants. When strike three is called, to the boos and hisses of fans, a great ballplayer realizes it's just part of the game.

In the game of life, we fall short. We get corrected and criticized. Those who succeed at playing the game of life learn from their mistakes and let them go. Failing at something does not make us failures; it gives us experience for the next time. People who are smart accept correction, learn from it, and brush it off.

God, help me to receive correction with grace. Let me see it as a tool to become better and realize that I will not grow without it. Once I take away the lesson, help me to let go of criticism. I pray others would see the change in my life that comes from a heart that is overflowing with gratitude for what you have done.

LETTING GO

Bearing with one another, and forgiving one another,
if anyone has a complaint against another;
even as Christ forgave you, so you also must do.

COLOSSIANS 3:13 NKJV

When someone hurts you, it can be really tough to let go of your frustration and forgive that person. Everything in you wants to maintain a firm grip on anger. *It's not fair,* you might think. *It's not right!* You want to hold on to the injustice of it all. But the Lord created forgiveness as a way to relieve a burden. Hanging on to that hardness of your heart is like hanging on to a pile a bricks that needlessly weigh you down.

Forgiving isn't easy. And letting go of your anger and hurt doesn't mean you're saying that what happened was okay. But when you stop being resentful it's as good for you as it is for the one you're forgiving. You may be surprised to find that you actually feel lighter after you've figured out how to let it go.

Lord, help me to forgive others like you've forgiven me. Forgive me for any resentment I've had. Relieve me of any burden I've carried in my resentment. I pray I'd be able to move on and let go.

JOY OF SALVATION

Restore to me the joy of your salvation,
and sustain in me a willing spirit.

PSALM 51:12 NRSV

There's an excitement that goes along with being a new believer. You overflow with joy, and you want everyone to know exactly what you're feeling. Over time, that initial feeling of excitement can fade. Eventually it can be tempting to be complacent in your relationship with the Lord. It's like it might have been once you were past an initial crush or the excitement of a new friend.

Sometimes you need to pray for protection over your relationship with the Lord. Pray that you'd come back to the same eagerness and enthusiasm you had at the beginning. Your relationship with God is meant to go the distance, not simmer hot then fizzle out. As you grow in your spiritual life, you'll learn more and more. That growth will sustain you for the long run.

Lord, thank you for the joy of your salvation. I want our relationship to grow strong and deep.

GUARDING THE BEANS

My children, we should love people not only with words and talk, but by our actions and true caring.

1 JOHN 3:18 NCV

There is a Bible story (2 Samuel 23:11-12) about a man named Shammah, who was one of King David's highly trained soldiers and personal bodyguards. Shammah was given a very specific task of guarding beans.

Shammah took his job seriously, though it might not seem like he was given a position of glory. And nothing could budge him from his beans. One day, the Philistines attacked. People ran for their lives, but not Shammah. He held his post, and he ended up slaying the Philistines, which resulted in a great victory.

What are you most passionate about? Your list might include faith, family, friends, hurting teens, human trafficking, the homeless, missions, and more. Now, think like Shammah, and guard your beans! Guarding your beans might include simple acts of service such as offering help, being a good friend, being kind, or putting others first. Sometimes, God calls us to do the radically ordinary. So don't fret over the grand acts you could be doing. God's greatest works can be done through everyday faithfulness.

Heavenly Father, help me to see with your perceptive eyes. Please help me to reach out to others in kindness and friendship. Let me guard my beans in everything I do.

THE PERFECT PROBLEM

Therefore, confess your sins to one another and pray for one another, that you may be healed. The prayer of a righteous person has great power as it is working.

JAMES 5:16 ESV

Have you ever been around someone who pretends to be perfect? They might flaunt their belongings, family, or station, and it can get annoying. No one is perfect, and the Bible has good news for us sinners. James 5:16 begins by telling us not to pretend we are perfect. We should share our struggles, weaknesses, and concerns so that we can pray for one another.

It's hard to admit our weaknesses. Start by finding someone who is a solid believer, someone who will pray when you ask them to. Sexual temptation, addiction, a broken relationship—whatever it is, prayer will release God's power into your life. You cannot do this by yourself.

It's hard to know if those perfect people are pretending or not. Either way, they are missing out on some pretty powerful prayer support. God came to set free imperfect people. Share, and faithfully wait.

Dear Lord, I am a little embarrassed at the thought of sharing private information, but I know I need your help. Please show me the right person to pray for me. Thank you for sharing the power of prayer with me and with your church.

DEEPER REVELATION

Jesus wept.

JOHN 11:35 NIV

"Jesus wept" is the shortest verse in the Bible, and that makes us want to dig a little deeper. Jesus' good friends, Mary and Martha, had a brother named Lazarus, who had just died. Jesus knew that he was about to raise Lazarus from the dead, so why did he cry?

Let's see if we can make some sense out of this. When a believer dies, Jesus knows that person is already cruising the streets of heaven. Perhaps Jesus weeps for the friends and family who are left behind. Jesus is familiar with heartache, and he weeps when we weep.

If we dig deeper still, there is another possibility for Jesus' tears. If we back up a bit in the passage, we see that Mary told Jesus that he should have come sooner. Everyone was wailing and weeping, and Jesus became "deeply troubled." Then, he wept. Jesus is God, and he was in complete control of the situation. Could it be that he wept because they did not trust him and his power fully? When we fail to trust Jesus, does he weep?

Father, please forgive me when I get impatient and want everything to work out according to my plan. Forgive me when I fail to trust you. Thank you for faithfully leading me through life.

18

STRENGTH TO TURN AWAY

We do not have a high priest who is unable to sympathize with our weaknesses, but one who in every respect has been tempted as we are, yet without sin.

HEBREWS 4:15 ESV

Do you ever feel like the Bible just doesn't apply to modern life? Or that God doesn't understand because he's a distant God who couldn't possibly get what's going on in your life? After all, you're faced with daily temptations, and there he is, up in heaven, unable to see what you're going through.

Here's the thing: God went through it all himself. The clothing styles may have been different and the technology certainly wasn't there, but Jesus Christ came to earth and faced the same things you do today. Greed, jealousy, lust—he saw it all. So he really does understand. Jesus knows what you're facing, because he faced it too—and won. You can look temptation in the eye and beat it, because you have Jesus in your life.

Lord, thank you for your empathy. Thanks for understanding where I am and walking through many of the same temptations yourself. Give me the strength to turn away from temptation today.

YOU BELONG

You, dear children, are from God and have overcome them, because the one who is in you is greater than the one who is in the world.

1 JOHN 4:4 NIV

Do you ever feel like you just don't belong anywhere? You might feel you don't fit in and that no one truly cares for you. That's a lie that the enemy wants you to believe. The truth is you are created by God. If you've put your faith in him, he lives in you and cares for you. And that means you belong. You belong to the best team you could ever imagine. It's the team that wins, and the team that's been formed out of love.

When you feel like an outsider, remember that you've been handpicked to be a part of the best. God wants you as an integral member of his team, and his Holy Spirit is in you, urging you on to victory over those that would bring you down.

Lord, thank you for choosing me for your team. I know I am created by you, and you are in me. I'm simply in awe.

DOWN IN THE PITS

Restore to me the joy of your salvation,
and sustain in me a willing spirit.

PSALM 51:12 NRSV

Do you ever feel down in the pits? How about overwhelmed, anxious, or depressed? It's exhausting, isn't it? Life has a way of throwing us into deep, dark holes. It might seem easier to stay put, right at the bottom of the pit, rather than try to climb out.

Let's think about the pits. Some pits are ones that we throw ourselves into. Gossip, addictions, bad choices, negative attitudes, giving up or giving in—these can throw us into custom-made pits. Other pits swallow us through no fault of our own. A tragedy, betrayal, difficult relationship, or illness can throw us into the abyss.

Have you lost hope? Do you feel like giving up? Don't miss out on what God has planned for you. There is work to do and lessons to learn at the bottom of the pit. Jesus meets us in our darkest place, and that's when we begin to understand how amazing he is. Grab hold of Jesus, and start new today. He will lift you up and give you a new direction, hope, and dream for your life.

Jesus, I feel like I have been fighting depression lately. Help me to toughen up and realize that life is not perfect. Help me to find support where I need it. Show me the next step in climbing out of my pit, so that I can find joy again.

QUIET WHISPERS

*In the same way, the Spirit helps us in our weakness.
We do not know what we ought to pray for, but the
Spirit himself intercedes for us through wordless groans.*

ROMANS 8:26 NIV

When it comes to prayer, it can feel awkward and forced. We want church-inspired phrases, but they slip out of our grasp. We aren't sure what is appropriate or inappropriate. We wrestle over our words, hoping that if we get it just right we will hear a resounding "Yes!" from the heavens. Kind of ridiculous, don't you think?

There is no right way to pray. Prayer is the quiet whisper of your soul: *Lord, I would really like to get that job; I'm looking for a miracle; I'm feeling down; I can't take it—I can't; Please show me how to handle this; Help me, Lord.* You get the picture. As we pray, we learn to recognize voice of the Lord as he quietly whispers words of wisdom and encouragement.

When we whisper our prayers, it opens the way for the Holy Spirit. He knows the yearnings of our souls, and he speaks on our behalf. He releases God's power; all you do is pray.

Dear Lord, you know my thoughts, and you understand my words. Help me to get into the habit of talking with you throughout my day, always listening for you. I want to know you better, Lord.

WALK THE TALK

If you are wise and understand God's ways, prove it by living an honorable life, doing good works with the humility that comes from wisdom.

JAMES 3:13 NLT

One of most common criticisms of Christians is, "They talk the talk but don't walk the walk." If a person claims to be a Christian and is judgmental, rude, heartless, or inconsiderate, it doesn't encourage others to sign up for the club.

Can a person be a Christian and act ugly? It's a good question. Christians can sometimes rely on "cheap grace," living as though grace gives them license to do whatever they please. They wake up in the morning, ask forgiveness, and do it all over again. But genuine faith doesn't look like that.

Jesus died so that we would be free *from* sin, not so that we would be free *to* sin. He didn't hang on the cross so we could keep doing what we're doing without feeling guilty. If we have truly made Jesus Lord of our lives, we will look different from the rest of the world. That little nudge in your heart is the Holy Spirit speaking to your conscience. Let's not neglect our actions; a poor walk can undo a lot of good talking.

Dear Lord, please forgive me for abusing your grace. Help me to be a light in the darkness. Let my life draw others towards you, not away from you, and may my life honor you.

TEMPLE OF GOD

Do you not know that your bodies are temples of the
Holy Spirit, who is in you, whom you have received from
God? You are not your own; you were bought at a price.
Therefore honor God with your bodies.

1 CORINTHIANS 6:19-20 NIV

When we accept Jesus Christ as our Savior, we are asking him to enter our lives and lead us in everything we say and do. As we mature spiritually, we walk closer and closer to him, making wise decisions in our daily choices. So why is it that we often forget that self-care is a part of that? So many times we choose to obey the Lord in other areas of our lives but forget one of the most important things—caring for ourselves.

God created us and formed us in his image. If *he* cares about us, *we* should care about us! That means getting enough sleep, eating healthy foods, exercising, and not giving our bodies to anyone or anything else that would displease him. He tells us that our bodies are his temples, and we should care for them as if they are worthy of that distinction.

Father, thank you for creating me. Help me to take good care of your temple.

DEPENDABLE

"For I hold you by your right hand—
I, the LORD your God.
And I say to you,
'Don't be afraid. I am here to help you.'"

ISAIAH 41:13 NLT

Did you know that the Lord would never lie to you? He won't lie because everything about him is truth. So when he flat out says that you have nothing to fear because he will help you, those aren't empty words. They're a promise, and he will see it through because his words are truth.

If you're afraid, reach out your hand to the one who loves you. He's ready to take it with a firm, yet gentle, grip. God is ready to pull you up out of whatever has you down. There is no need to fear, no need to worry, and no need to panic. He has it all under control and is always available to you. Depend on him. You won't regret your choice!

Lord, I give you my hand. Take it in your firm grip and help me through. Thank you for your truth. I know you will not let me down!

LIGHT OF TRUTH

You are to live clean, innocent lives as children of God in a dark world full of people who are crooked and stubborn. Shine out among them like beacon lights, holding out to them the Word of Life. Then when Christ returns, how glad I will be that my work among you was so worthwhile.

PHILIPPIANS 2:15-16 TLB

You, my friend, shine like a star. If you've got the love of Christ inside you, it's like a radiant beam that shines bright for all to see. You just can't help it. Let that light continue to sparkle by keeping close to God and following his Word of life and truth.

Even though circumstances around you might seem bleak, you stand out because you have Christ within you. People are drawn to you because of it. If you hold tight to the Lord's truth, his love and his light shine through you. Everyone who sees you will see his light too!

Father, I want to shine for you as a light. Thank you for your Word of life!

THAT'S VERY TEMPTING

We do not have a high priest who is unable to sympathize with our weaknesses, but one who in every respect has been tempted as we are, yet without sin.

HEBREWS 4:15 ESV

Thousands of years later, every story and every word of the Bible has something to say to each of us. In Matthew 4:1-11, we see the three ways that Satan tempted Jesus when he was alone in the desert, and we are tempted in the same ways.

Jesus was alone, tired, and hungry, and Satan tempted him to turn stones to bread. Satan begins by tempting us through our physical desires. Food, sex, alcohol, drugs—Satan starts here. But Jesus did not sin. Satan challenged Jesus to test God by jumping from the temple roof, relying on the angels to catch him. Satan knows us well. How many times do we test God by seeing how much we can get away with? But Jesus did not sin. Satan's last attempt was to entice Jesus to worship him in return for all the kingdoms of the world. Satan tempts us to ignore God and compromise our integrity for money, recognition, possessions, and glory. But Jesus did not sin.

Jesus understands, and he overcomes. He will provide a better way through temptation, and he will forgive our failures.

Dear Lord, help me to say no when I am tempted. The only thing that brings true happiness and fulfillment is a life with you. I know that, with your help, I can be free of Satan's hold.

SALTY

Be wise in the way you act toward outsiders; make the most of every opportunity. Let your conversation be always full of grace, seasoned with salt, so that you may know how to answer everyone.

COLOSSIANS 4:5-6 NIV

Jesus came to set people free, but he didn't force his way. He calls us to be witnesses and not judgmental or argumentative. We are called to be light, to be salt, but how do we share the truth about Jesus without being annoying? No matter what, non-believers can get mad when we talk about Jesus.

Some of us are too salty. Imagine biting into a juicy steak, only to find out that there is way too much salt. Too much salt makes people wince with distaste. If we pour it on as we witness, people will push away the message. On the other hand, consider biting into that same juicy steak with no seasoning. It won't make any impression on you. There needs to be just enough salt to enhance the flavor, and we need to be salty enough to enhance the flavor of Christ.

Be prepared for questions about your faith. Your words should be seasoned with grace and kindness. Shine your light to reveal his warmth and his love, but don't shine so bright that people close their eyes. The right amount of salt and light is appealing. People will want more.

Dear God, immerse me in your Word. Help me learn your truths so that I am prepared when I am challenged. Let my faith be balanced and bright, the kind that makes people want more of you.

FOR SUCH A TIME

You are a chosen generation, a royal priesthood, a holy nation, His own special people, that you may proclaim the praises of Him who called you out of darkness into His marvelous light.

1 PETER 2:9 NKJV

Do you ever feel afraid? The economy is shaky, jobs are scarce, college costs continue to sky rocket, people and countries seem to be more at odds with each other, families and marriages are falling apart—many people are afraid.

There is a Bible story about a woman named Esther, a queen by marriage to the Persian King. While Esther was living a cushy life with the King, there was an undercover plan brewing for the extermination of all Jews in Persia. Esther's uncle, Mordecai, got wind of this, and he asked Esther to make a plea to the King on behalf all of the Jews. There was just one hitch in Mordecai's plan; the King did not know that Esther was a Jew. This was a bit of a dilemma for Esther, but Esther's uncle asked her to risk her life, reminding her that she was born for such a time as this.

You, too, were born for such a time as this. You were chosen to be in this very place, in this time, to accomplish his purposes. He is always with you, and there is nothing to fear. You are part of his plan.

Dear Lord, help me to not be afraid. Like Esther, I must do the hard thing and stand alone when necessary. You have chosen me for this very time and place. Help me to fulfill my purpose and my call.

FIRST THINGS FIRST

You, dear children, are from God and have overcome them, because the one who is in you is greater than the one who is in the world.

1 JOHN 4:4 NIV

What is holding you back from accomplishing your dreams? We stand in awe at Christ's cross, but sometimes we forget what he can do in our lives. Our lives pale in comparison to our capabilities. Jesus paved the way to victory, yet sometimes we declare defeat before reaching the starting gate.

Maybe the Lord has been speaking to you about a certain matter, but you have ignored or overlooked his voice. Maybe you don't feel strong for a task. Maybe you have forgotten to dream.

We've got it backwards! We often try to overcome and achieve without the Lord's help. Seek him first, and the rest will follow. Then nothing can hold you back!

Precious Savior, is it really that easy? Forgive me for trying to achieve with my own strength. Help me to look to you rather than my own abilities. Lead me to seek you first and then taste the good you have in store for me.

THE THIN SPACE

We through the Spirit, by faith,
are waiting for the hope of righteousness.

GALATIANS 5:5 NASB

The thin space. Have you heard of it? As a spiritual term, it describes the mysterious place where people experience God. It's where you touch the edge of heaven. It's the moment when you know that you have heard from God and have been in his presence. It's like the place where the ocean meets the sky; you can't tell where one starts and the other begins.

Have you experienced it?

The Holy Spirit resides within us. Shouldn't we be able to operate in the thin space all of the time? It doesn't get much thinner than God inside of us. Are you missing out on the thin space, where heaven can reach your soul?

Dear Heavenly Father, I don't want to miss out on miracles. I am sorry for ignoring or not perceiving your presence in my life. Give me a taste of heaven so that I can grow and trust you more.

LIFE OF PEACE

Let the peace of Christ rule in your hearts, to which indeed
you were called in one body. And be thankful.

COLOSSIANS 3:15 ESV

From the time most of us were little, we were taught to be kind, tell the truth, and help others. But there's another thing we're also called to do—live in peace with each other. After all, we're all part of the same body, the group of believers that makes up the family of God. Peace comes from knowing Christ and allowing him to rule our lives.

Though the little sentence about being thankful seems tacked on almost as an afterthought, it is anything but that. Thankfulness, instead of complaining, brings people together. Thankfulness to God brings us closer to God. We can be thankful for everything he has given us, for everything he has done, and for everything he is. Let gratitude for him fill your heart.

Lord, thank you for calling us to a life of peace.
Help me to live that out in my life.

TROUBLE

"I have told you these things, so that in me you may have peace. In this world you will have trouble. But take heart! I have overcome the world."

JOHN 16:33 NIV

Some Christians believe that once they accept Christ as their Savior, life will become much easier. *Presto! Poof!* Like magic, pain and heartache will disappear and troubles will stop. But that simply isn't true. The world we live in is imperfect. Sad things and bad things will always be around.

That doesn't mean that there is no hope! Jesus is bigger than the world we live in. He has overcome it! Someday we'll live with him in a perfect place called heaven. But even now we can have joy regardless of what's going on around us. We can have peace because our hope doesn't depend on circumstances; it depends on him.

Lord, thank you for being my overcomer. Help me see past the troubles around me and feel your joy instead.

JOY IN OBEDIENCE

This is the love of God, that we keep his commandments.
And his commandments are not burdensome.

1 JOHN 5:3 ESV

Loving God means keeping his commandments. That doesn't mean you're saved because of what you do. No, you're saved by grace. Still, the works you do and choices you make are going to be an extension of who you are—a child of God. As his child, you'll want to follow him and the example he sets. You'll willingly choose to live by his instructions.

If you have a close relationship with God, his commandments won't seem like a burden. As you follow him, you'll be tempted less and less to do what *you* want. Instead you'll start wanting what *he* wants. Following his commands will become a joy.

Father, thank you for giving me your commandments.
I want to enjoy following them.

TRUTH AND SOCIAL MEDIA

A person who does not have the Spirit does not accept the truths that come from the Spirit of God. That person thinks they are foolish and cannot understand them, because they can only be judged to be true by the Spirit.

1 CORINTHIANS 2:14 NCV

Everyday online, individuals argue their case for truth. The Christian community has hot debates, articles, and posts over topics like gay marriage/traditional marriage, guns/no guns, pro-life/pro-choice—and the list goes on. Each side has compelling arguments. Which side is right? What is true?

When discussing the end of the age, Jesus warns us that many in the church will be deceived. Good and well meaning people will get it wrong. If we follow the guidance of someone who is deceived, we take a path away from God.

How do we know if someone is deceived? It's helpful to gather opinions from others, but you must always measure them against Scripture. Do not rely on someone else's interpretation of faith or the Bible. The best thing to do is to study the Bible and decide for yourself.

A little "truth tip" to keep in mind is that following Jesus rarely puts you in the popular crowd. In Matthew 7:13, Jesus tells us that the path to life is narrow.

What will be your ultimate source of authority—God's Word or the world?

Dear Lord, help me to not be deceived. Speak truth into the lives of those I love and help them to stay on the narrow path. Please lead me to discover your truth and stand on it.

FULFILLING EXPECTATIONS

Owe no one anything, except to love one another;
for the one who loves another has fulfilled the law.

ROMANS 13:8 NRSV

Are you ever overwhelmed by everyone's expectations? Sometimes, the pressure on young people is suffocating. The list of rules and expectations is long and exhausting, especially when you are faced with so many options and decisions. The desire to please others can be too strong, and it can distract us from what God expects of us.

God's list of expectations for you isn't cumbersome. His instructions are clear and simple, but all-encompassing: love one another.

If we set our hearts on loving one other, then we fulfill his expectations. We fulfill his law by living in faith. No matter what choices loom ahead, we can rest, knowing that we are obeying his will for our lives.

Jesus, help me drown out everyone's voices so I can hear yours clearly in the chaos. No matter where life may take me, may my focus be on obeying your commandment in all I do. Help me to love others.

MIRROR IMAGE

If any are hearers of the word and not doers, they are like those who look at themselves in a mirror; for they look at themselves and, on going away, immediately forget what they were like. But those who look into the perfect law, the law of liberty, and persevere, being not hearers who forget but doers who act—they will be blessed in their doing.

JAMES 1:23-25 NRSV

When you look in the mirror, what do you see? What defines you? Sports, friends, achievements, academics? If your identity is in anything but Christ, you will be like those who do not put their faith into practice. Your God-given passions may drive you, but without Christ, they will not satisfy.

You may not always like what you see in the mirror. Look again. You are holy, precious, and loved in God's sight. You are a beloved child, created in his image. Do not let other people define you or tell you otherwise. When you are tempted to compare yourself or your accomplishments with someone else, remember that God created you with a unique design for your life. Do not let the world dim the light that God has placed inside of you.

When you know your identity is that of a child of God, you will live like it. Do not grow weary of doing what he has called you to do. Go out into the world, be who God created you to be, and be blessed.

Dear Lord, forgive me for finding my identity in other things or people. Help me to live as a child of the living God. Thank you for loving me just as I am.

FEBRUARY

We are not saying that we can
do this work ourselves.
It is God who makes us able
to do all that we do.

2 CORINTHIANS 3:5 NCV

WISDOM IN WAITING

Everything is appropriate in its own time. But though God has planted eternity in the hearts of men, even so, many cannot see the whole scope of God's work from beginning to end.

ECCLESIASTES 3:11 TLB

The Lord loves us like crazy. He guides us, provides for us, and takes care of us. God has changed our lives for the better. He takes away the ugliness of our sin and makes us beautiful inside. He is open to us in every way, attentively listening to all our prayer. It's hard to imagine all that he has done or is going to do.

Sometimes, though, it seems like we have to wait forever for his answers. We want to know everything he has planned right this moment, but it's just not meant to be. Through waiting, we can learn patience, humility, and so much more. Being made to wait doesn't reflect a lack of interest or love on God's part. Rather, it's his infinite wisdom that keeps us close to him, learning to trust him even though not everything is clear.

Father, thank you that there's wisdom to be found in the waiting.

YOU ARE STRONG

It is God who arms me with strength
and keeps my way secure.

PSALM 18:32 NIV

No matter how big or small you are, you are a force to be reckoned with. That's because your strength comes from more than just your muscles. Your might comes from a place that is more powerful than any other on earth—God. He gives you strength and encouragement even when you feel it's hard to press through.

Keep your chin up, no matter what you're going through. You are strong. You've got God behind you. When you begin to doubt, just know that the Lord is right there, ready to fight for and with you. He believes that you are worth the fight!

Lord, I'm humbled by your willingness to stand with me. Thank you for giving me your strength when I don't have any of my own.

DELIVERED FROM FEAR

I sought the Lord, and He heard me,
And delivered me from all my fears.

PSALM 34:4 NKJV

Feeling anxious about anything today? Stop and take a deep breath. God knows how you're feeling and wants to meet you where you are. He will deliver you from what you're going through. The way he delivers you from your fears may not look exactly as you expect it to, but it will be perfect and just what you need. That's because his love is perfect, and he knows what's best.

When you feel like there is nowhere else to turn, know that you are never alone. The Lord loves you so much. He cares about the smallest details of your life, so think how much more he cares about big problems and anxieties. He will guide you through them all.

Father, I give you my fears. Please take them away. I'm seeking you and your presence today, knowing how much you love me.

GLOWING

The law of the Lord is perfect, reviving the soul;
the decrees of the Lord are sure, making wise the simple;
the precepts of the Lord are right, rejoicing the heart;
the commandment of the Lord is clear, enlightening the eyes.

PSALM 19:7-8 NRSV

Some people have something special about them. They almost glow from inside. That's the kind of beauty that following God's ways can give you. It's a beauty that can't be replicated or outdone by anything synthetic or put on.

The Bible tells that following the laws of God refreshes your soul. He can make you wise just by giving you the knowledge to do what's right. God gives you a lasting joy that surpasses any happiness. When you choose to walk with him, he makes you radiant. If you follow him every day, you'll stand out for your radiant spirit.

Father, I pray that I would follow you all the days of my life, seeking your joy and love.

I WILL NOT BE AFRAID

The fear of man brings a snare,
But he who trusts in the Lord will be exalted.

PROVERBS 29:25 NASB

The Bible tells us to not fear or be afraid 366 times. That's a fresh verse for every day of the year, including leap year—but is it a reasonable command? God doesn't guarantee anyone a happy or stress-free life. In fact, he promises that we will face trials and experience heartache. The belief that faith will always bring prosperity just isn't true.

However, God does not cause pain and disease; Satan does. Since the fall of Adam and Eve, Satan has roamed the earth, inflicting pain, disease, destruction, death, discouragement, and difficulty. Couldn't God put an end to our misery? Yes. He can, and he will. Presently, he allows storms to test our foundations so that we might see where we stand eternally.

Do not fear your tests. Fear will steal your joy. Turn your eyes heavenward, where your eternal home awaits. We may live twenty years or eighty, but from the perspective of heaven, we are one drop in the ocean of eternity. Invest in your eternal destiny.

Jesus, fear creeps into my life when I focus on the world. Help me to remember that this world is not my home. Earth is a place of preparation for what lies ahead.

HE HOLDS MY HAND

"For I hold you by your right hand—
I, the Lord your God.
And I say to you,
'Don't be afraid. I am here to help you.'"

ISAIAH 41:13 NLT

Think about holding hands. Maybe the hand is your significant other's. Maybe you dream about your crush taking your hand. Perhaps it's the hand of a child who is dear to you. Love, feelings of being protected, and other tender feelings arise when you hold someone's hand.

Today's verse tells us that God holds your hand. He is our dad in heaven, and he loves us more than we can imagine. Many Scripture verses describe what God does when he holds our hand. We're in good hands.

He goes ahead of you and is always with you. He makes rough places smooth. He leads the way, and he stands behind you. He seeks out a place for you to camp. He will humble your enemies as he fights on your behalf. He shelters you with his wings. He heals your broken heart and binds your wounds. He raises you up when you are down. He satisfies your desires. He is near to all who call on him in truth. He hears your cry and saves you. He watches over all who love him, and his right hand spreads across the heavens.

Lord, help me to remember your promises. I have nothing to fear. Thank you for your mighty hand that protects and guides my life.

44

IF YOU LOVE ME

It is the Lord your God you must follow, and him you must revere. Keep his commands and obey him; serve him and hold fast to him.

DEUTERONOMY 13:4 NIV

Do you love Jesus? We love Jesus in our hearts, but it's different from how we love those we can see and touch. In John 14:15, Jesus tells us that if we love him we'll keep his commandments. We aren't perfect, but this is the true test to see if we love Jesus.

When listening to a sermon or reading Scripture, it's easy to filter out which commands we aren't willing to keep. We close our minds and close up our Bibles.

Do you obey Jesus' commands?

Jesus, I do love you. Please give me the courage to follow all of your commands. Forgive me for cherry picking which commands to follow. Help me to submit to you as Lord over my life.

I CAN'T

Be strong in the Lord and in the strength of his power.
EPHESIANS 6:10 NRSV

Do you ever have a day when you just can't? You can't cope. You can't muster the energy. You can't face what is next, and you can't lift your spirits. You just can't do anything.

Think of your "I can't moments" as opportunities to see what God can do. When we pause for a moment, we can experience God in a tangible way. Sit yourself down and open God's Word. The book of Psalms is a great place to go when you feel like you can't. Over and over, David poured out his heart to the Lord because he couldn't.

Some of God's finest work is done in our weakest moments. His strength will be your strength. His joy will be your joy. Go with God.

Dear Lord, thank you for your powerful Word, which shows me that I can do all things through you, who gives me strength.

ANGER UNDER CONTROL

Be humble and gentle. Be patient with each other, making allowance for each other's faults because of your love.

EPHESIANS 4:2 TLB

When we're hot with anger, disappointment, and frustration, initially it might feel good to release our temper without restraint or a second thought. It's easy to feel justified with an angry reaction. But soon after we erupt, that good feeling doesn't feel so good. It's quickly replaced with regret and sometimes shame. Our anger can hurt us and the people we love.

We all feel anger from time to time; it's a normal and common emotion. But our anger doesn't have to control us. In those moments we have the God-given ability to resist our feelings of irritation and choose patience instead, ultimately choosing to love. Learning to take a deep breath, whispering a prayer, and meditating on Scripture are all ways that help us keep from giving in to anger. Focusing on God's goodness and grace makes letting go of anger much easier.

Jesus, fill me with your love for others. Teach me your patience and grace. I want to be quick to offer forgiveness, instead of quick to let my temper control my reactions.

CREATIVE SKILLS

He has filled him with the Spirit of God, with wisdom, with understanding, with knowledge and with all kinds of skills—to make artistic designs for work in gold, silver and bronze.

EXODUS 35:31-32 NLT

We see God's creativity around us in the unending sky, the deep blue oceans, the lush rainforests, and majestic mountaintops. We see his imagination in the creatures of the sea and in the variety of wildlife. As a master at his craft, God made us in his image. We are his best masterpieces. From our eye color to our personality, God designed everything with care and skill.

His creativity is everywhere—including inside you and me. God is creative, and he made us to be creative too. We all have different sets of talents and abilities that come from God. He loves the creative side of us, so we shouldn't stifle it, but embrace it. When we use our creative talent, we can use it with a heart of gratitude, good stewardship, and confidence.

God, your creativity brings me so much joy. Thank you for creating me in your image and giving me talents and abilities. Help me use those gifts today and every day for your glory.

TOTAL DEPENDENCE

"If you sinful people know how to give good gifts to your children, how much more will your heavenly Father give good gifts to those who ask him."

MATTHEW 7:11 NLT

Infants rely completely and utterly on their parents for survival. They are born trusting that they will be held, fed, and kept warm and safe. As they get older, though, they become more independent. As you become more of an adult, you may naturally feel as if you need your parents less. Still, there are huge questions about the future looming: Where am I going to college? Where am I going to live? How am I going to be able to provide for myself? The future can seem daunting as you try to figure out how you will set out on your own.

Even though you outgrow your need for complete dependence on a parent, you never outgrow your need for God. You don't have to have all the answers to your future. You can take comfort in knowing that God is a faithful God, he loves you, and he will provide for every need.

Jesus, as I get older, I pray I'd never grow away from you. I don't want to fear the future but trust in your tender care. May I depend on you for everything I need.

STANDARD OF PERFECTION

Let us then approach God's throne of grace with confidence, so that we may receive mercy and find grace to help us in our time of need.

HEBREWS 4:16 NIV

I messed up again. I can never get it right. Do these thoughts sound familiar? Sometimes the cruelest statements come from within us. They can be some of the most dangerous. Because we are human, we are bound to make mistakes, but that doesn't mean we should beat ourselves up.

Striving for perfection will only bring us down again and again. It is impossible and discouraging to live up to a standard of perfection. Instead we can be kind to ourselves just like God is kind to us. God views us with grace. When we do mess up, we can come to God, knowing he'll welcome us and pour his grace and love over us. He knows our hearts, and he forgives, readily and eagerly.

God, help me to see myself as you see me. Thank you for your unending kindness and grace. I am so grateful that you love me despite all of my mistakes.

ARE YOU SAFE?

You are to live clean, innocent lives as children of God in a dark world full of people who are crooked and stubborn. Shine out among them like beacon lights, holding out to them the Word of Life. Then when Christ returns, how glad I will be that my work among you was so worthwhile.

PHILIPPIANS 2:15-16 TLB

Most of us are familiar with the story of Noah, who built an ark and warned the people of God's coming judgment. His friends and neighbors thought he was crazy. Why? It's possible that it had never rained before, ever. Regardless of the theory, no one believed Noah.

Once the ark was finished, Noah, his family, and all of the animals climbed in, but the earth was still dry. The door remained open for one whole week. Noah warned the jeering and laughing people. On the seventh day, God himself closed the door. When the floods came, only Noah and his family were safe in the boat.

Jesus refers to himself as a door. He is our entrance to heaven. In Luke 13:25, Jesus tells a parable that sounds a lot like Noah's story: "When the master of the house has locked the door, it will be too late. You will stand outside knocking and pleading, 'Lord, open the door for us!' But he will reply, 'I don't know you'" (NLT). Do you know Jesus? Are you safe? The door is still open.

Dear Jesus, I want to live my life for you, no matter what the world thinks. Forgive me for neglecting to talk with you. Thank you that the door is still open.

NO GOOD REASON

My flesh and my heart may fail,
but God is the strength of my heart
and my portion forever.

PSALM 73:26 NIV

"Everything happens for a reason." Really? What reason could there possibly be for divorce, rejection, unemployment, abuse, cancer, or death? There is no reason. The popular coined phrase is simply that—popular. It is not biblical or accurate.

The Bible tells us, "in all things God works for the good of those who love him" (Romans 8:28 NIV). God's will is not pain; it's how we walk out pain. It's clinging to faith when everything has been stripped away. It's leaning on him as you put one foot in front of the other. It's relying on him to give you enough good that you can keep walking. It's when you choose to bring good into the pain. It's when you give others a reason for hope and for healing.

When there is no reason for pain, God is still good. Keep walking.

Lord, I see no good reason for what I am going through. Help me rely on your goodness. Give me the strength to walk this out and see your will.

HOPE WITHIN REACH

Yet what we suffer now is nothing compared to the glory he will reveal to us later.

ROMANS 8:18 NLT

When we're suffering, it is hard to believe that there's going to be an end to it. Sometimes the pain is so great, that it's hard to focus on anything else. Suffering often keeps us from seeing outside our current situation. Our perspective is shortened, and all of our senses are focused on what's happening right now.

God promises that joy will come. That joy will completely overwhelm any suffering we've had; there won't be any comparison. The pain and the heartache we feel on this earth is only temporary; it is not eternal. So in dark times, we can focus on hope. Hope that we will smile. Hope that we will feel no pain. Hope that suffering will end. Because God says so.

God, thank you for tomorrow. Thank you, Lord, that the pain and hurt I feel now is not forever. Thank you that your hope is always within my reach.

LIST OF IMPERFECTIONS

You are altogether beautiful, my darling,
beautiful in every way.

SONG OF SOLOMON 4:7 NLT

Ask anyone what they'd change about themselves and they're quick to pull out a list of so-called imperfections. We may criticize our weight, size, smile, hair color, or height. We may think we are dull and without personality. We may wish to be more outgoing and outspoken or wonder why we aren't smarter, stronger, or wittier. We compare ourselves to our self-created definition of beauty, and we feel like we aren't enough.

But we are. God created each of us. If we could only see ourselves the way God sees us, we would know just how beautiful we really are. There is not a hair on our pretty little heads that he doesn't admire. He loves our heart and our soul. He is proud to call us his own. Believe it, because it is true.

God, sometimes I don't feel so beautiful. It's hard not to compare myself to others. When I do, I just feel terrible. Help me see myself the way you see me, beautiful and loved.

SECOND CHANCE

"I will never again remember their sins and lawless deeds."

HEBREWS 10:17 TLB

Have you ever gone to bed at night just longing for a reset button? Maybe the day was just terrible, and you royally messed up. "If only I could start over again," you say.

You can. God's forgiveness gives you a new chance. Whether you ask forgiveness for a particular wrong or from a whole life of wrongs, he frees you from any mistakes. He doesn't keep a record of your wrongs. There is no list and no account to look back on. He is merciful and won't remind you of your shortcomings. God releases you of all sin and says that you are blameless. That's one grace-filled reset button.

God, I am so thankful that when I run to you for forgiveness, you give it freely. I am grateful that you cancel all of my debts. Thank you for each new day. Help me to embrace the new life you have given me.

BEING REAL

Clothe yourselves with humility toward one another, because, "God opposes the proud but shows favor to the humble."
1 PETER 5:5 NIV

In a world that often demands perfection, one of the hardest things to do is to be transparent with others. It's difficult to open up and reveal not just the good parts about ourselves but the broken parts that need attention and repair.

Authenticity is beautiful. When we can be real with friends about our shortcomings and faults, we give them the chance to usher in grace and compassion. We give them the opportunity accept us and encourage us. We find close friendships. Everyone struggles. We all have areas in our lives that need to be dealt with. We don't need to pretend to have it all together. Messy is ok. Messy is even beautiful. Messy is where God can begin working in our lives.

God, I want to live a life of authenticity. Help me set aside my pride and my desire for perfection. Give me the courage to be humble and bring to light the messy parts of me, so that I can embrace your grace freely.

DO YOU BLEND IN?

Do not be shaped by this world; instead be changed within by a new way of thinking. Then you will be able to decide what God wants for you; you will know what is good and pleasing to him and what is perfect.

ROMANS 12:12 NCV

There is a great deal of pressure in our society to look, think, and act the same. While also encouraging uniqueness, society pressures people to share the same beliefs, tolerances, clothes and fashions, lifestyles, politics, and morals.

Do you blend in? Does your life look any different from your friends? Do your friends know that faith is a priority for you? Believers should stand out, not by being obnoxious or self-righteous but by living a life that is better. We should look different. We should be more loving, more fun, more peaceful, more confident, wiser, and stronger.

When you march to your own beat, it can ruffle the feathers of those less brave. The crowd doesn't respond well when someone breaks away to forge new paths. That's okay—in fact, it's wondrous. Leave behind unhealthy behaviors, dysfunctional relationships, lies, and emptiness. God has a purpose and a plan for your life, and you will not fulfill it if you blend in. Choose to stand out.

Dear Lord, sometimes my lifestyle holds me back from my God-given potential. Help me to work past the status quo and move towards my future. Let me follow your footsteps.

PEACE IN IMPERFECTION

Let the peace of Christ rule in your hearts, to which indeed you were called in one body. And be thankful.

COLOSSIANS 3:15 ESV

Anxiety, frustration, depression, worry, sleepless nights. Is this your normal way of life? According to a recent study, 20 percent of millennials report being depressed, compared to 16 percent of baby boomers and 16 percent of Gen Xers. Forty-four percent of college students experience symptoms of depression. What is going on?

Current culture puts enormous pressure on young people. It causes stress in relationships and families while emphasizing image and success. One peek at any social media platform is enough to make you believe that everyone is more fun and successful.

Is it possible to have peace? Yes! Life will never be perfect; you must find peace amidst imperfection. Look with intention. The minute you feel a negative attitude brewing, pause. Stop whatever you are doing, and lay your worries and concerns on the Lord. Speak the words aloud. Then, crank up the worship music, and start thanking him for all the good things in your life—anything and everything you can think of. No matter what is going on in your life, you have access to God's peace.

Lord, I am feeling so stressed. I have been trying to fix my problems and plan my life on my own. I have done everything but trust you with this situation. I give it to you; I trust you. Help me choose peace.

RESET, REFRESH, AND RENEW

Therefore we do not lose heart. Though outwardly we are wasting away, yet inwardly we are being renewed day by day.

2 CORINTHIANS 4:16 NIV

Today's verse tells us that we are wasting away. All bodies die, and the world is slowly deteriorating. On the surface, life appears futile. We cannot escape things like corruption, pain, evil, betrayal, and death. If nature doesn't kill you, people will. Still, Paul tells us not to lose heart.

Reset your life by looking to the Lord rather than your circumstances. When life kicks your feet out from under you, drink in God's Word and be refreshed by the water of life. Dig into Scripture's treasures and unravel hidden mysteries. Read the passages over and over, until you are renewed.

Every single moment of your struggle is meaningful. Unseen by your eyes, it is preparing you. It is doing something, causing something, and it is good. Do not lose heart.

Dear Lord, I cannot find hope in my situation. Remind me that this life is a preparation for eternity. Lord, help me to trust you beyond human reasoning. I know that if I stay the course, I will one day reap rewards beyond imagination.

FRONT ROW FRIENDS

If we say that we have fellowship with Him and yet walk in the darkness, we lie and do not practice the truth; but if we walk in the Light as He Himself is in the Light, we have fellowship with one another, and the blood of Jesus His Son cleanses us from all sin.

1 JOHN 1:6-7 NASB

We have all kinds of friends. We meet some through shared activities and events. Some are the ones you hang with on the weekends. Above all, there are friends who have earned the right to a front row seat in your life.

Front row friends stick with you. You know each other's stories and shared journeys. No matter what comes, you can count on front row friends to support and encourage you. Your friendship is comfortable and irreplaceable. It is critical that your front row friends are believers. Believers inspire you to be better, and they always want the best for you. They are the friends who pray for you. Front row friends are ones that God chose for you. Save their seats.

What kinds of friends do you have? Do some suck life out of you? Do they draw you away from your faith? Do you find yourself trying to fit in? Galatians 1:10 tells us that we should not try to win everyone's approval. If we are constantly trying to please our friends, we cannot please God.

Jesus, it's easy to spend too much time with the wrong friends. I find myself compromising my relationship with you. Instead, let my friendships reflect my faith in you. Thank you for my front row friends; let me pray for them now . . .

NOT DEFINED BY THE PAST

It is for freedom that Christ has set us free. Stand firm,
then, and do not let yourselves be burdened again by a
yoke of slavery.

GALATIANS 5:1 NIV

Too often we let our past define us. We may be ashamed of choices we made or the life we lived before following God. The things that used to be can blur the new life we have.

You aren't defined by your past. Whoever you were or whatever you did before God gave you a new life is irrelevant. God gave you freedom. He gave you a new identity. So when you tell your story, you can say with confidence, "I was saved by grace." God is the light in all your stories, even the darkest ones. His grace and name redefine you. Take hold of the freedom he wants you to have.

God, I am so humbled that you've freed me from my past. Thank you that I'm not defined by what I was. Help me embrace the new identity you've given me.

STAYING PURE

Run from sexual sin! No other sin so clearly affects the body as this one does. For sexual immorality is a sin against your own body. Don't you realize that your body is the temple of the Holy Spirit, who lives in you and was given to you by God? You do not belong to yourself, for God bought you with a high price. So you must honor God with your body.

1 Corinthians 6:18-20 NLT

Sex. You see it glorified everywhere—on TV, in music lyrics, on billboards. The message is that sexuality is something to put on display. By staying pure, you are led to think you are missing out on the most exciting thing ever. The truth is that your sexuality is something to be protected, honored, and saved for the right time and the right person.

Sex is amazing, but it was created for marriage. Outside of marriage, sex leaves you unguarded and vulnerable. God doesn't want you to wait to have sex because he wants to deny you fun and pleasure. Rather, he wants you to wait because he knows how painful an intimate experience can be at the wrong time. He wants to protect you from unnecessary harm. He has your heart in mind when he says, "Wait."

God, sex is a gift worth waiting for. Help me to stay pure in a world that encourages sexual relationships outside of your perfect plan. Give me patience to wait and strength to protect my purity.

RELEASING WORRY

"Don't worry about these things, saying, 'What will we eat? What will we drink? What will we wear?' These things dominate the thoughts of unbelievers, but your heavenly Father already knows all your needs."

MATTHEW 6:31-32 NLT

Worry is a heavy burden to carry. Worry can cause us to lose hope. It damages our spirits and our spiritual, mental, and emotional health. The more we worry, the more it can grow and affect all our relationships, including our relationship with the Lord. It is a burden that the Lord doesn't want us to own, which is why he tells us again and again to bring all our worries to him.

Why continue to wrestle with worry when we don't have to? We don't have to exhaust our hearts and spirits. Trusting God is the answer to getting rid of anxiety. He is the only answer for complete freedom and peace. When we feel anxious, we can go to the Lord and he promises to fill us with peace and understanding.

Lord, you tell me to release all of my cares and burdens to you. Thank you that you guard my spirit, heart, and mind from worry. I'm grateful that I can cling to your promises. I trust you.

BROKEN

Do not fear, for I have redeemed you; I have summoned you by name; you are mine.

ISAIAH 43:1

If something is broken, we often set it aside to collect dust in the garage, or we simply throw it away. After all, if something is broken it doesn't have much value. Half the time fixing the item isn't worth the added cost and effort.

You might feel like you're too broken to be fixed, that whatever you've done is too bad and that you're beyond repair. You may feel too broken inside to be worth fighting for. God thinks differently. God takes the broken and the hurting and saves them. He sent Jesus to redeem you. That means, he valued you so highly that he sent Jesus to die on the cross. He loves you too much to set you aside.

God, thank you for loving me so much you sent Jesus to show your love. Thank you for seeing my value and redeeming even the darkest and messiest parts of my life.

PRAISE FROM SOMEONE ELSE

Let someone else praise you, not your own mouth—
a stranger, not your own lips.

PROVERBS 27:2 NLT

Ever met someone who is constantly telling others how awesome they are? Listening to them can get annoying and old in a hurry. The Bible says that it is better for others to praise you for something you did well than to brag about it yourself.

There is always more satisfaction when others take notice of us on their own than when we work to make them notice us. One person who notices is Jesus. Who better to be praised by? The day is coming soon when he will look at those people who have loved and obeyed him and reward them. Instead of bragging about yourself, give praise and glory to Jesus.

Lord, help me not to brag. Instead, help me to look for ways to please you. I want your recognition more than anyone else's.

VOICE OF CONVICTION

My guilt has overwhelmed me
like a burden too heavy to bear.

PSALM 38:4 NIV

Do you ever have moments where your conscience won't leave you alone? You've said some nasty things about someone, or you looked at something you shouldn't have, and it doesn't sit well in your heart.

God cares enough about you to bring conviction and the Holy Spirit's nudging. His objective is for you to repent because, until you do, your sin will cause a wall between you and him. God cannot stand separation with you, so he will do whatever it takes to break down what gets in the way of your relationship. When you begin to feel that conviction come over you, respond to it quickly and with a humble heart.

Keep my heart soft toward you, Lord. I don't want to ignore your Holy Spirit. Sometimes I try to push away that voice of conviction, but I want instead to be thankful that you're willing to make our relationship right.

MARCH

He has granted to us his precious
and very great promises, so that
through them you may become
partakers of the divine nature,
having escaped from the
corruption that is in the world.

2 PETER 1:3-4 ESV

OVERCOMERS

"I have told you these things, so that in me you may have peace. In this world you will have trouble. But take heart! I have overcome the world."

JOHN 16:33 NIV

It's not easy to be a young Christian in the "crazy Christian" club. Many young believers resort to a quiet private life to avoid criticism and confrontation from their peers. Are you afraid to admit that you follow Jesus? Do you shuffle around like a second-class citizen?

My friend, you are a citizen of heaven. You have won, not lost. Take a hold of what is already yours—the amazing power that rose Jesus from the dead. That power is always available to you. When you are weary or heartbroken, it is there. If you are struggling with poor relationships, unemployment, or addiction, it is there. The creator of the universe, who created the mountains and the ocean, created you for a specific purpose; you cannot and will not fail.

Yes, it will be hard. If it was easy, you would not have to call on the Lord, and you would not experience his mighty power if you never cried out. You can do this. Square your shoulders; lift your chin. Not one person can destroy you. You have victory in Jesus, and you will overcome.

Dear Lord, sometimes I walk as if I've lost the battle of life. Remind me to call on your power, which brings hope, healing, and new life. Thank you for dying, so that I could have abundant life.

OUTWARD FOCUS

Serve one another humbly in love.

GALATIANS 5:13 NIV

Don't you love it when someone says, "Here, let me help you," or "Can I do anything for you?" It's wonderful to be on the receiving end of servanthood. Being served gives us a sense of being loved and cared for. When we are going through time of sadness or discouragement, it can be hard to stop looking at our own needs and see the needs of others. Pain often makes us focus inward.

We learn to know God's love more deeply through serving. If we ask God to open our eyes to those hurting around us, he will. Pushing aside our own needs and problems and offering a helping hand to someone else will make our struggles fade. Serving others gives us a greater perspective—God's perspective—and brings us inexplicable joy. God uses us to show others how much they're loved, and then he fills us with purpose.

Lord, open my eyes and heart to those around me who are hurting. Use me as your servant to show them your love. Use me to bring others comfort and joy. May my own struggles teach me compassion and empathy.

ARMS OPEN WIDE

He was despised and rejected—a man of sorrows,
acquainted with deepest grief.

ISAIAH 53:3 NLT

High school can feel like a popularity contest. Lines are clearly drawn in the sand defining who is popular, liked, and accepted. If you don't make the cut, it can be utterly devastating. Being rejected is one of the worst feelings. We feel like we're on the outside, aching for approval and acceptance. We all long to fit in. We all desire to belong, to have a place, to feel included.

Some of us don't feel like we belong anywhere. We don't fit in with our peers often because of our beliefs and life choices. We begin to wonder what is wrong with us and why no one loves us. If you find yourself in that hard place, Jesus will meet you there. He knows intimately what it's like to be rejected. In him you will always belong. When others turn their backs on you, he is there waiting, arms open wide. As a child of God, you belong, you have a family, and you have a place in God's home. When you seek to be with him, he won't turn you away. He loves you.

Lord, I feel at home with you. I feel wanted, loved, and accepted. Your love comforts me and fills the loneliest places of me.

INTIMACY WITHIN MARRIAGE

A man leaves his father and mother and is joined to his wife, and the two are united into one.

GENESIS 2:24 NLT

Sexuality isn't something to be embarrassed or ashamed about. God created our sexuality. Sex was his idea. Unfortunately, the world peels away the sanctity of sex layer by layer. It gives us the impression that sex is something casual, leading us to believe that we can enter into the sexual relationships we want and walk away without getting hurt.

It's simply not true. Sex outside of marriage ruins our view of it and brings heartache. Sex inside the context of marriage brings joy and life. God created sex to be between a husband and a wife, to bring unity and oneness to their marriage. It binds them together through intimacy and trust. Sex within marriage is beautiful, sacred, special, and worth waiting for.

Thank you Jesus for creating my sexuality. Thank you that I don't have to feel embarrassed or ashamed about the way you made my body. Help me honor you by protecting my body, not taking it for granted or abusing its purpose. Give me the strength and patience to wait for the gift of sex inside marriage.

CONNECTION

You make known to me the path of life;
in your presence there is fullness of joy.

PSALM 16:11 ESV

Have you ever had a conversation with someone and walked away feeling like that person never heard what you had to say? Sometimes we're so distracted with media that we actually fail to connect with the person sitting right beside us.

We all long to connect with others on a deep level and talk about what's really important. That describes how God feels about spending time with us. God is always willing and ready to be with us. But sometimes we get caught up in being busy. If we put down our gadgets, quiet our hearts, and take turns speaking and listening, we discover what it means to have a deeper relationship with him.

Jesus, thank you that you enjoy my company. I'd like to enjoy your company more too. Time with you is refreshing and exactly what my soul needs.

BEST FRIENDS

I love the Lord, because He has heard
My voice and my supplications.
Because He has inclined His ear to me,
Therefore I will call upon Him as long as I live.

PSALM 116:1-2 NCV

Who is your best friend? Be it a parent, old friend, or significant other, it is someone you spend time with. All good relationships require communication. We communicate differently with our best friend than we do with our neighborhood barista or mechanic. You tell a best friend everything, good and bad. You share intimate details of your lives with each other, expecting a listening ear in return.

What about God? Do you rattle off meal and bedtime prayers, or do you share your fears, hopes, dreams, worries, achievements, and embarrassments—everything that is whirling around in your soul? A relationship is always growing or decaying; there is no in between. If you have slipped into a routine of three prayers a day and church on Sundays, you may find your relationship with Christ joyless.

What is the remedy? Talk to God again, about everything and anything. Spend time with him every day. Let your relationship grow, and you will experience the joy of your Father opening up his heart to you, too.

Father, I desire a relationship with you! I open my heart. Please, draw me close to you.

CLICHÉ ANSWERS

Do not fear, for I am with you; do not be dismayed, for I am your God. I will strengthen you and help you; I will uphold you with my righteous right hand.

ISAIAH 41:10 NIV

When facing difficulties, cliché sayings can cut deeper than they can help. They leave you wondering if anyone really understands what you are going through. Does "Do not fear " seem like that to you? Inside, we are screaming, *God, do you really see what's happening down here?* Heartache, sickness, bullying, hate, loneliness, insecurity—all of these hit hard in dizzying combinations. The world's problems are vast and even more overwhelming. How can we not fear?

God isn't giving our deep hurt and struggle an impossible, cliché answer by saying, "Do not fear." He goes on to say, "I am with you . . . I am your God."

The limitless God is always with you. He will give you courage, lift you up, and let you soar. He will help you conquer every fear and overcome every trial. Even bitter struggles are tiny in comparison to eternity. When you finally see them for what they are, you can move forward in God's strength. Don't dismiss him as trite or uncaring. He wipes away every tear and knows every temptation. His care goes infinitely beyond what you can imagine.

God, draw me close to you. Be my refuge. Let me know your nearness, and strengthen me to face the world without fear.

MUSCLE MEMORY

This is the love of God, that we keep his commandments.
And his commandments are not burdensome.

1 John 5:3 ESV

God is not cruel, but years in an unhealthy church or family environment can mold the voice of Jesus into one not his own. How do you read his voice? When his mother, Mary, tells him that the Canaan wedding party is out of wine, how does his response sound? Is it condemning and annoyed, or kind and passionate?

What about the many stories of Jesus healing people? Does he heal with a sigh of exasperation? Does he gather the little children into his arms with frustration and eye rolling? Of course not!

Neither is he harsh towards you. He loves you. If you practice and train in that love, like an athlete toning muscle, you will slowly realize he is justice and love, not cruelty. He does not respond to you annoyed, angry, frustrated, or irritated. If that is how you are reading his voice or hearing his response to your prayers, you're stuck in a rut of wrong thinking. He wants his voice to be a support for you, not a burden. Like the dedicated athlete, one day it will come naturally, and you will hear his true voice.

Jesus, I know you love me. You do not give me the law as a burden but as straight paths and right ways for my feet. Let me hear your true voice, the source of all love and compassion.

FINDING YOUR WAY BACK

Repent and return, so that your sins may be wiped away, in order that times of refreshing may come from the presence of the Lord.

ACTS 3:19 NASB

Arguments and gossip can divide friendships. In the same way, sin divides us from God. It creates distance between us. That's because God is holy. Sin makes him sad because it means we can't be near him. We can't stand in his presence when we have grieved his heart.

Separation from him, though, doesn't have to be permanent. Because he loved us so much, he provided a way back to relationship with him through grace. Finding our way back into his presence and into his forgiveness is as simple as reaching out and asking for it. What he asks for is a genuine heart of apology and the willingness to return to him. Telling him we're sorry and asking his forgiveness, we welcome him to refresh us with his presence and to redeem us with his grace.

Lord Jesus, when I do things I know aren't pleasing to you, my instinct is to run. I don't want to stand before you ashamed. Clean me from the stain of my sin and make me new again in your eyes.

LIVING NOW

For still the vision awaits its appointed time;
it hastens to the end—it will not lie.
If it seems slow, wait for it;
it will surely come; it will not delay.

HABAKKUK 2:3 ESV

The growing up years can feel like a holding pattern. You're standing right on the brink of your whole life, but it's still just out of reach. It's easy to start wishing away the time and looking ahead to when your future will really start.

But all we really have in life is the present moment. None of us are promised tomorrow. If we spend our days planning for the future, then we'll look back and see only a list of plans instead of a life well lived. God wants to use us right now, as we are. He doesn't ask us to change, grow up, get married, or get older before he can use us. He asks us to embrace today, this moment, and obey him with our whole heart.

Offer your life up to God, as it is, and let him take care of the details. He will create for you the most beautiful life.

God, I want to live for you right now. Help me to give you every moment. I want to live my life with your vision and your purpose.

BEING FAIR

Treat others as you want them to treat you.
LUKE 6:31 TLB

"But that's not fair!" How many times have you heard that? How many times have you said it? No one likes to be treated unkindly, but it happens to all of us. We get hurt by someone and feel angry or frustrated. Before we know it, we've turned around and treated someone else that same way.

Treating others unfairly will never fix how we've been treated. The only way we can fight evil in this world is to do good. We have to be intentional in our relationships and stop to consider our words and our actions. That's when we'll be able to show Christ's love. By making a change in the way we treat others, our kindness will become contagious. We'll create an environment where the love of Christ is shared freely.

God, I've been treated unkindly many times and sometimes feel like taking it out on others. But you've put your love in me, and I don't want to give anything less in my relationships. Help me to be kind.

WHAT ARE YOU DOING?

Work at living in peace with everyone, and work at living a holy life, for those who are not holy will not see the Lord.

HEBREWS 12:14 NLT

"What are you doing with your life?" Everyone is compelled to ask, and graduates grow weary of hearing it. The pressure is on to have an answer. Shouldn't we all have our lives perfectly planned after school? Career, marriage, number of kids, where to live, how high of an education to pursue—such decisions can feel immediate and necessary.

Perhaps our goals and bucket lists are off base. What if what was most important was not what you are going to do, but who you are going to be? Jesus doesn't call us to have successful careers, large homes, or lovely family Christmas cards. Yes, he might bless you with such gifts, but he is more concerned with how you will represent him. Do you live for him? Does his light shine in all you do?

It's difficult to keep the graduate question from defining you. Set your eyes on the true-life goal—living a peaceful, holy life. It's not a resume-builder, but you will be far richer in the age to come.

Jesus, help me not to get caught up in the questions of success. Help me define myself and my life by your Word. Reassure me of your will for my life, even when everything is uncertain.

TASTE AND SEE

O taste and see that the Lord is good;
How blessed is the man who takes refuge in Him!

PSALM 34:8 NASB

There's not much better than a delicious meal. Close your eyes and picture your favorite foods all laid out on a table. What would be there? A juicy steak? Creamy pasta? A sushi platter? Chocolate cake? Whatever you picture, it's nothing compared to the feast that God has for you. It's not a feast of food but a feast of all that's good. And what's really good is spending time with *who* is good. Having a relationship with the Lord "tastes" better than anything you've ever known.

The best part is that you can indulge in spending time with God whenever you want, day or night. Taste and see that the Lord is good. He's the best, and he wants to share with you all that he is and all that he has for you. He is so generous that way.

Lord, I want to taste all the good that you desire for me, desiring you above all else, and taking refuge in your love.

WEIGHT LIFTED

"I will forgive them for the wicked things they did,
and I will not remember their sins anymore."

HEBREWS 8:12 NCV

When someone has done us wrong, it's hard to forgive much less forget. We've got long memories when it comes to the injustices we see in our lives. Thank goodness that's not how the Lord operates! He loves and forgives us. When we confess we're wrong, he forgives us and makes is as though we'd never sinned at all. Everything is wiped clean. He doesn't hold onto the list of our failings for future reference.

Knowing that gives us freedom. We don't have to be weighed down under guilt from the past. It's as if God has taken a huge weight that was pressing down upon us, and lifted it right off. There is no need to punish ourselves over and over. He's forgiven and forgotten.

Lord, thank you for forgiving my sins. I praise you even more for forgetting them entirely, wiping them from my history. I am constantly amazed by who you are.

A BEAUTIFUL PLAN

Lord, you are my God;
I will exalt you and praise your name,
for in perfect faithfulness
you have done wonderful things.

ISAIAH 25:1 NIV

If you filled up a book with all the good things about God, the pages would never end. He is good, kind, loving, generous, just, and fair. While it might not like seem like that sometimes (after all, the world of full of bad things), God is faithful and walks alongside us in tough times as well as good times.

He has a beautiful plan for your life. But he won't force that plan on you. Instead he loves you by giving you a choice—to follow his plan or leave it. He knows his plan is best. It bubbles up from a heart that loves you deeply and knows you intimately. Will you trust him?

Lord, thank you for knowing every detail of my life and caring enough about me to plan each step.

GIFT OF MUSIC

Let the word of Christ dwell in you richly, teaching and admonishing one another in all wisdom, singing psalms and hymns and spiritual songs, with thankfulness in your hearts to God.

Colossians 3:16 esv

Every small detail of your life should be done in the name of Christ Jesus. You can praise him with every fiber of your being. You can be thankful to him for the richness of all the blessings he gives. When you hear his Word, you can soak it in and let it take over. You'll be rewarded for doing so, since you'll experience life in fuller way.

One of the ways God gives us to praise and thank him is through psalms, hymns, and worship songs. Music is also a great way to learn Scripture. Putting melody to a verse is one of the best ways to memorize it. Through music we lift God up and celebrate who he is and what he's done.

Lord, thank you for the gift of music. I want to sing your praises all day long, telling others of your great goodness.

ALWAYS WELCOME

If we confess our sins, he will forgive our sins, because we can trust God to do what is right. He will cleanse us from all the wrongs we have done.

1 JOHN 1:9 NCV

God tells us again and again that if we confess our sin, forgiveness is ours. Sometimes shame, pride, and even fear hold us back from coming to the Lord and asking for what he has already promised. We stand at the doorway of his home, not sure if we are welcome.

But we are always welcome! We never have to give in to hesitation or embarrassment or be afraid of his response. God is everything a good father is. He is kind, forgiving, and gentle. He won't refuse our request for forgiveness, because there's nothing more he'd like than to have a close relationship with us.

Jesus, when my fear or my pride stops me from coming to you, draw me in with your kindness. Thanks for never turning me away. Thank you for washing me clean and making me new again.

TWO WAYS OF MERCY

My eyes are ever on the Lord,
for only he will release my feet from the snare.

PSALM 25:15 NIV

We all make stupid decisions, right? Many define their teenage years with rebellion and regretful decisions. Thankfully, there are two ways that God delivers us.

First, he provides ways out of temptation. He might warn you through a friend or pastor. He might set roadblocks in front of us to keep us from a stray path. And he may even allow hard times and trials that are grace in disguise. Second, he delivers us out of the trap. We will end up in traps, because we still have our sinful natures alongside our new natures. When we fail and find ourselves trapped in the snare of sin, God provides ways for us to get out, be they ladders of support or ropes of prayer. Above all, he forgives us of our sin.

Our God is full of mercy! You need only lift your eyes to the Savior and call on his name.

Keep me from the snare, Lord, and let me see the warning signs before I fall. When I do fail, release me, forgive me of my sin, and let me dwell in your presence again.

DITCH THE SAMPLES

O taste and see that the Lord is good;
How blessed is the man who takes refuge in Him!

PSALM 34:8 NASB

Many people experience the good things of God. The sun rises on the righteous and the wicked, after all! And God's creation is displayed to all, and isn't there goodness to be found in a butterfly's wings, a sun-dappled forest, or a mountain top view? There is goodness in children's laughter, a hug from a friend, and the satisfaction of your favorite dessert.

These are the good things available to all. As a child of God, you know there is so much more. The world is a store, displaying little carts of samples. The greatest good comes when you take the sample into your home and make it a meal.

God wants you to come to the table and feast on his goodness. You thought you knew about his love, from the sun on your face to the refreshment of rain, but your he wants to give you the gift of Jesus and to lavishly display his goodness. The beauty of the banquet is it never runs out. For his children, his goodness and mercy abound forever. Instead of wandering around the store, picking at the samples, come home to his bountiful table.

I want to taste that you are good, God! I want to experience the goodness you have stored up for those who call upon you. You are good and abounding in love, and I thank you for that truth.

DON'T RUSH

Lead me in your truth, and teach me,
for you are the God of my salvation;
for you I wait all day long.

PSALM 25:5 NRSV

Have you ever wished life was more black and white? Which school to attend, which job to get, even which type of pizza to eat—so many decisions and so many that need to be made in such short periods of time. When time is crushing, how do you make those tough decisions?

A good rule of thumb is that God is in no rush. He is the creator of time. He holds it in his hand and is in complete control of the universe around you. To him, one day is a thousand days, and a thousand years is one day. The God who can stop the sun mid-track does not need to hurry up!

If you are making a decision and feeling rushed, remember that even though our culture is fast-paced and pushy God has perfect timing. Next time a decision looms, pray for direction but also look around and see how much pushing is happening to make this decision work. Let his peace and timing come to you, and remember that he works for your benefit.

Jesus, slow me down. Let me be in step with you. Thank you for your Holy Spirit, who guides and provides wisdom.

THE PERFECT FIT

True godliness with contentment is itself great wealth.

1 TIMOTHY 6:6 NLT

In a culture where we're constantly bombarded with images of things that we want but don't have, things that we didn't know we needed but are told we do, and things society says we should have, it's easy to feel discontent.

True contentment doesn't come with having a nice house, a swimming pool, an iPhone, or even great friends. Real satisfaction comes from being true to yourself and living the way God intended you to. You were made in God's image, so walking in his ways is like slipping on the perfect size shoe. It fits right and feels right because it is.

Jesus, help me to be content with who I am and what I have. When I start to feel restless, help me find contentment in being with you and doing what's right.

WHAT ABOUT ME?

"Rise and stand upon your feet, for I have appeared to you for this purpose, to appoint you as a servant and witness to the things in which you have seen me and to those in which I will appear to you."

ACTS 26:16 ESV

From the time you were little, parents and grandparents, teachers and friends probably asked you, "What do you want to be when you grow up?" Someday you might grow up to preach in front of thousands, or find a cure for a deadly disease, or build an orphanage in Africa.

Sometimes defeat and self-doubt worm their way into your life, and you might begin to wonder if your life has meaning and purpose. It can seem as though others are called to great and amazing things, and you are left wondering, *What about me?* Right now, your calling is pretty simple: study hard, listen to your parents, love others, serve others, and make an impact in everyday ways. Your calling may seem small in your eyes, but to God there is great purpose even in the little things that don't bring a lot of fanfare. You are an important part of his plan, so embrace every day and impact people in the ways that you can.

God, keep me from wasting my time and energy searching out a bigger, more important calling. Help me seize the calling you've given me today—to love and serve those around me.

DO THE IMPOSSIBLE

The Lord is my strength and shield.
I trust him with all my heart.
He helps me, and my heart is filled with joy.

PSALM 28:7 NLT

Have you ever set your heart on doing something only to be discouraged by the careless words of others? They may have felt that you were inexperienced or ill-equipped. Sometimes people have good intentions but aren't particularly helpful.

Too often we let other's disbelief in our abilities keep us from pursuing our biggest dreams and desires—desires that God has planted in our hearts. If they think we can't, then we shouldn't, right? Wrong. Often God calls us to do things that seem bigger than ourselves. Sometimes he calls us to do the impossible because he believes in our abilities. Other times he calls us to do the impossible because he wants us to lean on him. Instead of letting self-doubt grow, our confidence should be in him.

God, help me place my confidence in you, not in the opinion of others or the circumstances around me.

GREATNESS

God thunders wondrously with his voice;
he does great things that we cannot comprehend.

JOB 37:5 ESV

We all have dreams for what we want out of life. Most of us aspire to greatness, even though we can't see how it will happen. Greatness cannot grow on its own; true greatness comes from God. That's because God is the one who is great.

His voice commands the thunder, creates light, and dawns the day. It's through his strength that our lives will count for something greater than we can imagine. Put your life in his hands. Allow him to speak to your soul. And watch what he will do with your life.

God, you know that I desire greatness. I look around me and I see that everyone is living for something—some of it matters and some of it doesn't. But I want to live a life that is set apart. Marked by your call. Use me to do great things.

THE GOOD WIFE

An excellent wife, who can find?
For her worth is far above jewels.

PROVERBS 31:10 NASB

Why do you think a good wife isn't easy to find? More importantly, what do you think an "excellent" wife is?

Marriage is a life-long commitment. While it isn't always easy, marriage is one of the greatest gifts God gives. Though being a wife and being married may seem a long way off, you can start preparing now. Purposefully grow yourself in grace, in forgiveness, and in humility. Keep your heart free from entanglement with other loves. Practice forgiveness. Become a natural at apologizing. Learn to speak with kindness, even when you want to speak in anger. Let your heart be guided by the Lord, and trust that he will give you a great marriage in a world of so many broken ones.

God, I know that I can trust you with my heart and my future marriage. You created love and want us to love one another in a way that reflects the love you have for the world. Do a work in my heart now so that my marriage will forever reap the benefits.

STAY CLOSE

Dear friends, let us love one another,
for love comes from God.
Everyone who loves
has been born of God
and knows God.

1 JOHN 4:7 NIV

It's a simple principle: The closer an object is to a light source, the more illuminated that object will become. Stay close to the light of Christ, let him shine through you. Draw your love from him. Without being connected to him as your source, your light will go out and you will find yourself empty.

When our love comes from God, who is love, it is being replenished every time we step into his presence. He loves others through us, and he will never run out of love to give. Always love—above everything else. Love Christ first, and then those around you. The moment you begin to love others more than you love Christ is the very moment your light will go out.

Love through me, God. Shine your light through me. I'm too weak to do life on my own. I have to be connected to you as my strength, my light, and my love.

TITLE SELF TALK

Praise the Lord, my soul, and forget not all his benefits—
who forgives all your sins and heals all your diseases,
who redeems your life from the pit and crowns you with
love and compassion,
who satisfies your desires with good things so that your
youth is renewed like the eagle's.

PSALM 103:2-5 NIV

Do you ever talk to yourself? Maybe you look in the mirror and say, *I can do this!* You might call yourself stupid when you mess up or mumble reminders and directions. Internally, we talk to ourselves all the time, and sometimes those voices get confusing. What direction is from the Lord? What is not? What is true? What is false?

Have you ever written down ways the Lord has blessed you? Grab a notebook or your phone and give it a try. Ways you have been set free from sin? Write them down. Ways you have overcome sickness and health issues? Write them down. Have you been satisfied and renewed in his presence? Write it down.

When waves roll and the voices are deafening, remember your list. All through the Old Testament, God asks the Israelites to remember. We, too, are called to be people who remember God's promises. Remembering silences the voice of the enemy, steadies us, and directs us to look to our refuge.

Thank you, God, for all you have done for me.
Let me always remember your goodness!

CONDEMNATION VERSUS CONVICTION

*"I will forgive them for the wicked things they did,
and I will not remember their sins anymore."*

HEBREWS 8:12 NCV

Even if we do get trapped in a snare, God is full of grace. This verse is fitting for the morning after a fall. Have you ever experienced a morning after? You wake up with extreme regret at a decision made, a sin committed.

Hebrews is the perfect pick-me-up, a warm cup of coffee in your moment of despair. If you have repented of your sin, what you are feeling is condemnation. The enemy wants you to dwell on your failure so that you feel trapped and useless. The enemy's condemnation fools us into thinking God will never forgive us or use us again. The Holy Spirit, on the other hand, convicts us of sin. This is also painful and sorrowful, so it can be confusing.

However, conviction ends in grace. If you are convicted and repent, you know that God has removed your sin. You are righteous and blameless before God in the blood of the Lamb.

Free me from condemnation, God, and from the snare of sin! Continue to convict me and bring me near to you and your grace.

SCIENCE LESSON

He is before all things, and in Him all things consist.

COLOSSIANS 1:17 NKJV

Although science has progressed in leaps and bounds since the writing of Scripture, we still do not know how everything works. Quick science lesson, even though you've just graduated: there is something that physicists call "strong force," which holds the nuclei of atoms together. The repulsive forces between the positively charged protons would drive the nuclei apart without it.

There are three other universal forces: gravity, electromagnetism, and the weak force. You can look up all these things yourself, but the real lesson is this: what is holding our world together? And here's a better question: who is holding your world together?

The answer is God the Father, God the Son, and God the Holy Spirit. God created the world and holds it together. Rest in the comfort that God has the power to control our world, its course, and your life.

Oh God, you created the universe and hold it together. Thank you for your sovereignty over the entire universe and over my life.

GOD'S WORD, MY LIFE

Sanctify them in the truth;
Your word is truth.

JOHN 17:17 NASB

So much of this season of our lives is about preparation. We're constantly preparing for something—for graduation, for college, for a career. We're looking forward, and we want to be ready for whatever lies ahead.

As we lay the groundwork for our lives, we can't exclude the best thing—God's Word, which is truth. If it's not woven throughout our life's plan, then everything we've worked for amounts to nothing in eternity. In his Word we will find the key to so many of our questions, to our peace, to our being worth something. Take hold of God's truth. Learn to long for his wisdom. Open his Word every morning. Take in what he has for you and weave it in to your life until you can't go a day without it.

Teach me to love the Bible, Lord. I don't want to do life without your wisdom; I need your truth. Speak to me and help me be excited to open your Word.

THE WORTH OF KINDNESS

Be kind to each other, tenderhearted, forgiving one
another, just as God through Christ has forgiven you.
EPHESIANS 4:32 NLT

Kindness is always worth something. Meanness may come more easily at times, but it's never the right choice. We can't know the full picture by just looking at someone. We have no idea what's going on in their lives. Everyone has a story. Everyone has issues, struggles, and hurts. The reality is that the only safe bet is to be kind. Simply put: treat others as you want to be treated. Smile, be friendly, and be caring. Better yet, find out what someone's story is.

The reality is that *you* don't always deserve kindness. Sometimes you act in a way that isn't worthy of someone's best. But Christ gives you his best always. He always loves you, forgives you, and comforts you. There's no mistake in being kind. By showing kindness to others, you will always be doing what's right.

Thank you, Jesus, for your kindness. Help me think past my own circumstances and recognize that everyone has a story. I know that kindness is never the wrong reaction to someone. Help it to always be my first.

APRIL

The Lord directs the steps of the godly.

He delights in every detail of their lives.

Though they stumble, they will never fall,

for the Lord holds them by the hand.

PSALM 37:23-24 NLT

BECAUSE OF HIS MERCY

*Then he saved us—not because we were good enough
to be saved but because of his kindness and pity—
by washing away our sins and giving us the new joy
of the indwelling Holy Spirit.*

TITUS 3:5 TLB

Do you ever feel like you have to earn friendships with people? Like if you don't dress a certain way or talk a certain way or have certain things you won't make the cut to be their friend? Sadly, that's the way it sometimes works. Some checklists make you attractive, popular, or deserving.

God doesn't operate that way. We didn't do a thing to earn his salvation. God saves us because of his love for us. There's nothing we did to earn it. There is so much freedom in realizing that. When we know that his mercy has never been about what we do, we learn to relax and accept it.

Thank you, God, that I don't have to earn your mercy or your salvation. You are so good to me. I'm so thankful for your mercy. In a world where I have to prove myself again and again, you're merciful just because that's who you are, not because of anything I do.

GOD IS THERE

I cried out, "I am slipping!" but your unfailing love, O Lord, supported me. When doubts filled my mind, your comfort gave me renewed hope and cheer.

PSALM 94:18-19 NLT

Life is full of ups and downs, victories and failures. Many times we feel great, and life is going well. Then there are moments when our foot slips, and we find ourselves losing balance. Sometimes we're on top of the world; other times we're ready to give up. We don't always feel strong.

It may seem like God is more present when things are going well. But even at our lowest, God is there. His love is unfailing, and it will support us through the darkest times. Don't be afraid of your own doubts. God is big enough to renew your hope and to restore your faith. He will walk with you through the darkest times and rejoice with you through the greatest.

Thank you, God, for being there for me always—when things are at their best and things are at their worst. When sadness comes over me, bring me joy. When worry takes over my mind, give me hope. When I'm happy, join me in celebrating.

COUNTING TIME

Set your minds on things above, not on earthly things.

COLOSSIANS 3:2 NIV

Ever heard the phrase, "put your money where your mouth is"? Let's change it up bit: "put your time where heart is . . ."

If you want to properly assess your priorities and what captivates your heart, write out your schedule. Where do you spend your time? Do hours slip by on TV shows or computer games? Are you captivated by looking and waiting for that next like or comment? Can you spend hours at the gym but aren't sure where your Bible is?

One of the enemy's greatest strategies is distraction. He pleases us with little things like the praises of others. Sometimes, he distracts us with material goods. If you think that every Christian's great downfall will come from some monumental sin, think again. It's daily activity and a gradual decline that pulls us into the grave. Take careful inventory of the hours you get every day, and analyze what is eternity-driven and what will be burned up like straw at the end.

Jesus, my time is a gift and so precious. Help me get rid of the chains of little distractions that bind me so that I can give every moment to you.

AS WE GO

Everything is appropriate in its own time. But though God has planted eternity in the hearts of men, even so, many cannot see the whole scope of God's work from beginning to end.

ECCLESIASTES 3:11 TLB

As Christians, we know it is our duty to take the gospel to the world—to our neighbor, our city, to our nation, and to the ends of the earth. While this is an exciting commission, evangelism often seems more like a burden. We take the responsibility for others' belief upon our own shoulders, saddling our souls with the weight of others' eternal destinies.

Take refuge in the truth. Whose responsibility is salvation? It's Jesus' and his work on the cross. It's the Holy Spirit and his conviction of people's hearts. Consider yourself a simple messenger. All you are asked to do is speak.

Do your part in God's work as the messenger. Ask God to free you from fear and stir up his passion for eternity inside you. Ask God what your role in the Great Commission is, whether you should go, pray, or send to the harvest. All of us are called to witness as we go, making disciples and evangelizing to all around us.

Dear Lord, sometimes the enormity of your commission feels too heavy. Remind me that I only carry your message. Give me the strength to live as a witness, and show me what to do.

DOORS

"My thoughts are nothing like your thoughts,"
says the Lord.
"And my ways are far beyond anything
you could imagine."

ISAIAH 55:8 NLT

Graduation is a critical time. You desperately want to know that you are hearing God's voice clearly. It is not an easy task, especially in the heat of a situation, to discern his voice from emotional reasoning. God knows all the doors, and he holds every key. He opens impossibly locked doors, and he also gently closes them.

After facing closed doors, it can be difficult to move, but God has not forgotten you. He goes before you, makes paths straight for you, and opens new doors. Perhaps God keeps a door closed because he wants to change your heart, not your space.

Success is not measured outwardly in the kingdom of God; it's the work being done within your soul that matters most. What you see as a sure success could be an inward step backwards. Trust in God, let him know your thoughts and fears, and ask him to open the door that will bring him the most glory.

God, I know your ways are higher than mine. Help me to trust in you when I don't understand the doors before me.

FIGHT SMARTER, NOT HARDER

You provide a broad path for my feet,
so that my ankles do not give way.

2 SAMUEL 22:37 NIV

As far as salvation goes, the work is done. On the cross, Jesus paid for every sin, conquering death by rising from the tomb. You are free.

As you walk the Christian path through life, you may feel less than free. Doubt may creep into your mind, telling you to work harder, faster, and stronger for your salvation. Keep this sentence constantly before your eyes: there is no way you can add to your salvation.

That doesn't mean you should sit back and coast. God will often ask you to step up and fight, and he will make your feet rock solid and show you the right path. Remember that you do not fight alone. God wants to strengthen you in your weakest areas so that you can succeed over your enemy.

Jesus, thank you for going to the cross for my complete salvation. Thank you for fighting for me; give me the strength to fight for you.

CLIFF JUMPING

It is God who arms me with strength
and keeps my way secure.

PSALM 18:32 NIV

"The struggle is real." Catchy phrases have short life spans, but they often ring true. How can you look up to God when the earth below your feet is unstable? The bravest thing you can do is to trust in God's goodness.

When you first look up from your feet, it feels like you're walking off a cliff. The future is nothing but fog. You are not sure if you landed that job, were accepted into that school, or if the doctor is going to give your family member a clean bill of health. You aren't even sure if there is anything under that fog once you leap into it!

Let God strengthen you. The future is already a reality to him. Cope how you need to: cry it out, pray, or speak with friends and family, but remember that the future is an already established truth. Don't sit on the edge, waiting to feel strong or waiting for the fog to lift. Jump into his goodness, and you find the strength to rise up. He will keep you secure. What are you waiting for? Jump!

God, you are my strength. Help me to stand up and walk out in that truth.

WORD WOUNDS

When I was in trouble,
I called to the Lord,
and he answered me.

PSALM 120:1 NCV

Why is King David so distressed? Someone lied about him. In this psalm, David is struggling with keeping his reputation, with lies being spread about him. David's first instinct was self-defense. He wanted to take up his own cause, but he knew better. He knew that God would hear his pleas and defend him.

Sometimes, it is best to remain silent. Words wound deeply and take a long time to heal. Your reputation may be at stake, but know that God will fight for you. If you have acted with integrity, lies will dissolve in the end. There are few things in life harder than this silence, but God can move in that silent space. Let prayer be your noise, and pray for yourself and your enemy.

David's distress ended in the knowledge that God would defend him from his enemies. You, too, can stand confident. Even though slander cuts deep, God will defend you. You need only ask.

God, these words spoken against me have cut deep. Help me bridle my tongue and not speak against them, allowing you to come to my defense.

SOARING HOPE

May the God of hope fill you with all joy and peace as you trust in him, so that you may overflow with hope by the power of the Holy Spirit.

ROMANS 15:13 NIV

Have you ever built up all your expectations and hopes into something, only to be disappointed? Perhaps, at your tenth birthday party, that toy you wanted wasn't in the wrapping paper that you tore open. It may seem trivial now, but as a kid, it was a big deal! Eventually, after enough of these let downs, you learned to adapt your expectations, lowering them.

Take heart! You don't need to do that with God. Your hope is based on the unshakable, unchanging perfection of his character. Your hope is so perfectly guaranteed that you have God himself, the Holy Spirit, with you at all times. He will never disappoint you or let you down.

No matter what you face, be filled with joy and peace. Let your hope soar. He will never let you down.

Oh Lord, sometimes my heart can get discouraged. My hope has been disappointed so many times that I fear to hope again. Help me soar to new heights with my hope secure in you.

MONSTERS

I sought the Lord, and He heard me,
And delivered me from all my fears.

PSALM 34:4 NKJV

When we are young, fears are tangible or immediate: fear of heights, fear of the dark, fear of lurking monsters in the closet or under the bed. Then, we learn Bible verses like Psalm 23, which talks about "fearing no evil." That evil becomes personified in our imaginations, looking more like the boogieman than like the sin in our lives.

However, as we grow older, evil looks less like a boogieman and more like the monster of the flesh inside each of us. No one is righteous. We are all born with a sinful nature, even from the moment we first cry out into this world. Sin is evil, and whether it is evil against us or evil we commit, we can fear its effect or power.

But God is our deliverance! When it seems like we cannot go on and our world has stopped because of evil, he is our hope. He has conquered all of sin's power, and he holds the keys over sin and death. This sinful world can be an ugly and terrifying place, but God is so beautiful. He promises that anything he touches will be made new and beautiful.

I praise you, Jesus, for overpowering death and the grave. Help me to not fear evil, knowing that you are with me. Please protect and guide me, and remind me of your promises.

FENCES ON THE PATH

I have hidden your word in my heart
that I might not sin against you.

PSALM 119:11 NIV

As a child, making friends is as easy as a game of tag. In high school and college, we band together by mutual interest or space with clubs, dorms, and classes. We may hold onto these friends for a long time or keep up with them on social media. Either way, as years go by, our friends will experience the joys and sorrows of living in a broken world, and it may change them.

Past Christian friends may make choices or follow doctrines that hurt your heart. The one, true path is narrow. The longer you live, the more clearly you will see how narrow that path is.

Take heart! Psalm 119 is the fence on either side of this narrow path. Knowledge and study of Scripture is the compass you need to navigate life. Do not be fooled into thinking the Bible is outdated or irrelevant—it is the most relevant book to cross your hands. In a culture of wide roads peppered with potholes, stay on the narrow path!

May your Word be ever before my eyes, Lord! Let neither me nor my friends be led astray but keep us grounded in and guided by your Holy Scriptures.

LUNCH

Now to Him who is able to do far more abundantly beyond all that we ask or think, according to the power that works within us, to Him be the glory in the church and in Christ Jesus to all generations forever and ever. Amen.

EPHESIANS 3:20-21 NASB

There is a little boy whose mom packed him an ordinary lunch. Then, Jesus walks in with five thousand of his hungry friends, plus women and children, and asks his disciple, Philip, where to buy food. If only we had the response to this question, because eight months salary wouldn't cover this party! The next disciple, Andrew, brings forward this little boy and his little lunch. He hands the tiny bread loaves and fish to Jesus with one hand. Perhaps with the other he shrugs and asks, "What can you do with this?"

Jesus is ready to meet you where you are. Maybe all you can muster is a tiny lunch, or maybe you showed up to the party with faithless, empty hands. Either way, seek God's face and understand that he is calling you to something. Don't say no simply because you think your lunch is too small for the task. Bring what you have, and let God be God.

The lunch story starts with five loaves and two fish and ends with twelve baskets of leftovers. How will your story end? Hand it all over to God.

Jesus, I give you what I have. Remind me that you can move mountains with whatever I bring.

WE HAVE NOT ARRIVED

The law of the Lord is perfect, reviving the soul; the decrees of the Lord are sure, making wise the simple; the precepts of the Lord are right, rejoicing the heart; the commandment of the Lord is clear, enlightening the eyes.

PSALM 19:7-8 NRSV

Finally, I have arrived! Have you ever felt like this? Maybe this is how you feel right now, upon graduation. Some people live in a world of "if I can": *If I can get this job; If I can move to this area; If I can date this girl; If I can . . .* Subconsciously, that sentence often ends with the phrase, "then I have arrived."

It is wise to not fall into that trap in our earthly lives, and even more important in our spiritual lives. Maybe you are thinking if you just get baptized, go to a certain church, pray enough, or walk with the Lord long enough, you will have arrived in your Christian walk.

The Christian life is just that—a walk. It is a repeated process of repentance and forgiveness. That is why King David writes that his soul needs reviving so often! Christianity is not a static state but an ebb and flow of restoration and renewal as we grow closer to Christ. Complete sanctification won't happen until we reach heaven, so avoid the prideful feeling of having arrived.

Jesus, thank you for walking with me through life, refining me and reviving my soul. Breathe new life into me and continue to show me how to become more like you.

BORING CHRISTIANS

Make a joyful noise to the Lord, all the earth!
Serve the Lord with gladness!
Come into his presence with singing!

PSALM 100:1-2 ESV

What was the lie that Satan told Eve in the garden? It was a smear campaign against the goodness of God. You've seen similar campaign ads on TV, taking words out of context and picking apart wrong moves to spread rumors and doubts about their opponent.

Today, the smear campaign against God continues, and people buy into it. The modern lie is that God takes away all our fun and makes life boring. Many Christians don't give people a reason to doubt this! It seems we have banned the "joyful noise" portion of this psalm from inside the church walls. We are called to confess God's goodness. Consider the cheers at a sporting event. We are on the winning team! Why not shout and proclaim it aloud?

Are you ashamed of being a Christian? Has Satan stolen your joy and made you a part of his smear campaign against Christ? If so, pray that God would restore your joy of salvation and help you shed fear of others' opinions. Share his goodness with all around you.

Lord God, fill me with your joy! Help me to see where I am ashamed of you. I repent of that shame, and may I never pass up an opportunity to sing your praise.

QUIET BRAVERY

Lord, you are my shield,
my wonderful God who gives me courage.

PSALM 3:3 NCV

Bravery is rarely loud and flamboyant. It is a deep breath before the plunge. It is open hands lifted to our faithful God. It is gritted teeth, sure hands, and a quiet resolve to move forward. Bravery is a humble strength, rarely sparkling in the spotlight but always rich in character.

You may view people cliff jumping or sailing the Atlantic as very brave, and that is true. True bravery, however, rests in those who daily walk in God's goodness. They trust him with each breath, and they completely surrender themselves to his shield and strength. They are not the ones you would pick out of a crowd as strong or brave, but God moves mountains through them.

Be brave when the world around you is shaking. Rely on God. It is better to face a raging storm with Jesus than a calm day without him. Let him shield you from fear, and he will strengthen you.

Lord, I want to follow you bravely. Help me resist fear.
Shield me from it, and let me face life with quiet resolve.
You are the strength within me, and I thank you for your
presence.

CELEBRATE

Lord, you are my God;
I will exalt you and praise your name,
for in perfect faithfulness
you have done wonderful things.

ISAIAH 25:1 NIV

You did it! The long journey is over. Homework, sleepless nights, worry, stress, juggling school and activities—you overcame them all. Did you ever want to quit? Where there times you thought you wouldn't make it? Yet here you are, on the other side. You've made it through the mountains and successfully completed this journey. Congratulations!

Today, take a moment to list what God has done for you these past few years. Remember every heartache overcome, every test passed, every game won—all the moments of God's faithfulness. Thank and praise God for each item on your list. You can do it verbally and loudly. Throw a party if you want to! Your friends and family might throw you a graduation party, so throw God a party, praising him for his thankfulness.

Give credit where credit is due. Praise him!

Thank you, God! Thank you for moving in all of these situations. Thank you for your faithfulness. Thank you for saving and redeeming me for your purpose!

TUNE YOUR DAY

Because your steadfast love is better than life, my lips will praise you. So I will bless you as long as I live; I will lift up my hands and call on your name.

PSALM 63:3-4 NRSV

There is a proper order to a concert. Players tune their instruments before they play. What an awful cacophony would result if musicians tuned their instruments at the end of the concert! What beautiful harmony would be missed because of the lack of order!

Like a guitar or violin, our lives need daily tuning. To walk in harmony with God, we have to tune before we play. Each day is a concert. Do you prioritize time in your morning to tune? Prayer is an essential start to your day. In prayer, you can submit your schedule and demands to God and ask how he is moving today. Maybe he wants to slow down or speed up the day's song. Maybe he has picked a completely different tune than you expected. How would you know if you wait until the end of the day to tune? We want our lives to be beautiful melodies and that means listening for God first.

What do your mornings look like? Can you roll out of bed five minutes earlier to give him time? Turn off the car radio and pray instead? Have your Bible near so you grab it first instead of your phone? What morning habits will help you tune to God?

My life is not my own, God, and I want to play in your concert. Show me how I can align my day with you every morning.

STILLING CHAOS

"Be still, and know that I am God;
I will be exalted among the nations,
I will be exalted in the earth."

PSALM 46:10 NIV

When you picture this verse, what do you see? A person meditating in an open field with green grass below and blue skies above? That is beautiful and motivating, but check out the context of Psalm 46. David writes about the earth giving away, mountains falling into the sea, war between nations, and kingdoms collapsing. The scene from your favorite apocalyptic movie is probably not what came to mind for "be still!" However, that chaos makes God's command more meaningful.

Psalm 46 is a picture of the disorder and uncertainty of our current culture, politics, and personal lives. Knowing that God is in control of all things stills the chaos. We know that every knee will bow and every tongue confess his name. Our faith hits the pause button on that apocalyptic movie, silencing the intense music, and then our friend, the Lord, tells us how the movie ends.

You can be still and not worry about the world, because you know what happens in the end. God wins.

God, the world is an unstable place, and sometimes fear threatens to overpower my faith. Remind me of your perfect and good control, and let me be still in your presence.

PICK YOUR PEOPLE

Let the word of Christ dwell in you richly, teaching and admonishing one another in all wisdom, singing psalms and hymns and spiritual songs, with thankfulness in your hearts to God.

COLOSSIANS 3:16 ESV

Friends are some of God's greatest gifts to us. Graduation means parting ways with people you saw almost every day. Late nights, early mornings, endless cups of coffee, holidays, study sessions, tests, stress . . . all that time has grown into relationships you don't want to leave. Perhaps you are on the opposite end of the spectrum, longing for new faces and a fresh start in the friendship arena.

Wherever you are, "pick your people." Adult men and women have to work hard to make meaningful connections after graduation, be it high school or college, especially once spouses and families enter the picture. Still, you need your people. You need advice, comfort, and joy from more than just your significant other or family. You need friends to belly laugh with, friends to travel with, and friends to just watch movies with after a bad day.

Adults can ignore the need for friends. Pick your people, sniff out possible friendships, and pursue them! Encourage them, invite them over, and invest your time. It takes work, but you are rewarded with companionship in the storms of life.

Jesus, thank you for the friends you have placed in my life. If there is a lack of meaning in my friendships, point me to those I can consider "my people" so we can run the race towards you, together.

GIFTS IN SERVICE

Earnestly desire the greater gifts.
And I show you a still more excellent way.

1 CORINTHIANS 12:31 NASB

What are you good at? What are your gifts? All graduates consider these questions as they finish one phase of life and enter the next. They want to make sure they get the most out of the next step. While some gifts are harder to find than others, seeking them out is not a problem. There are plenty of quizzes online to help with that, both silly and serious. What we need to seek and desire are gifts that will benefit others as we serve in them.

The problem is wanting gifts that bring us meaning, fulfillment, or acknowledgement from others. The "more excellent way" is serving in love. Seek out your gifts, perhaps take one of those quizzes, and then focus on using them to serve others in patience and kindness.

When the focus becomes less about gifts and more about service, God's love shines brightest.

God, thank you for making your church a body comprised of different gifts. Reveal to me what mine are, and help me use my gifts to serve your body in love.

CLOSE TO HIS HEART

*Let us not become weary in doing good, for at the proper
time we will reap a harvest if we do not give up.*

GALATIANS 6:9 NIV

Be close enough to Jesus that you feel his heart beating
for the nations. The world is large, and the mountain of human
suffering and needs can seem insurmountable. It paralyzes
us to a point of doing nothing at all. The weariness of doing
good is the fear of not doing any good, or the fear of not
conquering all. But we aren't asked to conquer all. Christ
already conquered all! We need only be compassionate.

What is compassion? In Hebrew, the word comes from
the origin word *rechem*, which means womb. Like a mother,
we carry compassion inside of us for the hurts and sufferings
of others. It's not just a check or a quick, "Praying for you!"
Instead, we enter into their suffering and carry it.

The key is not to rely on our strength, which fails quickly,
but to be close to Jesus and his power. Then, the suffering is
a bridge to the arms of a loving Savior. Compassion, fueled
by constant closeness to the heart of Jesus, is the vehicle we
need to reap the harvest. Remain close to him and be the
womb for those around you.

Lord Jesus, help me not to tire of compassion or become
afraid of the suffering of this world. I want to roll up my
sleeves and jump in. Remain close, so I can feel your
heartbeat. Show me who needs compassion.

ONE SIMPLE VERSE

If we confess our sins, he will forgive our sins, because we can trust God to do what is right. He will cleanse us from all the wrongs we have done.

1 JOHN 1:9 NCV

As a general rule, picking the Bible apart verse by verse is a bad idea. It can take advice or stories out of context, tailoring God's Word to be what you want. However, if there was ever a verse to take out and hold on to, 1 John 1:9 would be it. It contains a simple truth: we are sinners.

The verse starts by saying we need to confess sin, which implies that sin happened. It's time we called sin what it is. It is not a disease, mistake, or lifestyle but death that separates us from God. But that's not the end of the verse! Once we confess, he forgives. His perfect faithfulness means perfect forgiveness, and he desires a relationship with you! He doesn't want you separated from him, which is why he made a way for us to draw near to him in confession.

Trust him when he says that nothing is too bad, too big, or too awful to separate you from his love. Don't let sin remain hidden, pulling you into its darkness. Confess, bring sin to light, and then dwell in that cleansing light.

Jesus, I confess my sin to you now. I want to walk in the light as you are in the light. Let nothing remain hidden!

ARE YOU CONTENT?

Keep your lives free from the love of money and be content with what you have.

HEBREWS 13:5 NIV

As a new graduate, the world is at your fingertips. Opportunities abound. Success cries your name, beckoning you to come grab hold. The American dream is defined as prosperity and wealth, the core foundations of our culture.

Is that how God's economy works? The love of money is rooted in desire for power, comfort, security, and pleasures. These aren't necessarily bad, but when we search for them apart from God, we end up worshiping status and wealth to hide the discomfort of what is really going on in our hearts.

Do you rely on God for your daily bread? Do you trust him to care for you, free of worry? Do you have a life of thankfulness that stems from contentment? Pursuing happiness through love of money and the world's economy will leave you with nothing in the end. Trusting God to be your security, comfort, and status will bring rewards in heaven beyond imagining. Where does your heart lie? Keep your heart content, and let God overflow your cup.

Oh God, help me not be distracted by the riches, power, and comfort of this world. I am just a sojourner, spreading your gospel. May my rest, comfort, and security always be in you. I repent of my discontent heart; train me in contentment.

YOU ONLY LIVE ONCE

Do not be deceived: "Bad company ruins good morals."
1 CORINTHIANS 15: 33 ESV

It's true that we only get one earthly life, but there is another life after death. There will be a resurrection of the dead where we will be judged as either followers of Christ or unbelievers.

The Corinthian church was in danger of being led astray by short-term theology. What dangerous theologies are in our world today? Jesus warns that good people in the last days will be deceived by those close to them. Be careful of which voices and avenues shape your worldview and speak into your life. Let Scripture weigh and test every thought and idea.

You can be a catalyst for change by speaking God's true Word, but there will be many who want to drag you down with their own personal theologies. Stand firm on the Word of God, and do not let yourself be swayed by popular opinion or corrupt, deceived company.

Jesus, thank you for winning us eternal life on the cross. Help me to recognize deception and alert me to the wolves that lurk about. Let me stand firm on your Word.

I WANT TO BE LIKE YOU

Be humble and gentle. Be patient with each other, making allowance for each other's faults because of your love.

EPHESIANS 4:2 TLB

You probably like people like you. What's not to like? You have great taste, after all! Sports teams, clothes, interests, age— similar interests help us bond. However, we do not get to pick the body of Christ. God created each and every human being, and he desires that everyone be a part of the body of Christ.

Other Christians are different from you. The body of Christ varies in political views, cultures, favorite sports teams, favorite foods, and so on. Sometimes, differences can be annoying, but God desires his bride to be unified.

There is no requirement that other believers worship like you, pray like you, or do outreach like you. The only requirement is God's call to every believer to contribute their specific talents and gifts. In this call, we are also asked to bear with one another's quirks. Easier said than done, but we are all working towards the same goal. It is not easy to be a part of the church, but it is on this bumpy road that God refines us to be less like us and more like him.

God, I want to love the church—your body—the way you do. Help me cast aside judgment and instead bear Christ's burden with my brothers and sisters.

WORLD SERIES CHAMPIONS

We say with confidence, "The Lord is my helper;
I will not be afraid."

HEBREWS 13:6 NIV

In 2016, the Chicago Cubs won the World Series after a 108-year drought. Naturally, celebratory flags and banners covered the city. One church sign read, "Cubs win—God does answer prayer!" What about fans of the opposing team, the Cleveland Indians? Their fans were probably praying, too! Who had their prayers answered?

It's hard to confidently say that the Lord is our helper when we feel we are losing. We may wonder if we are playing for the wrong team. Disasters crash into our lives, and we wonder if God really wants to help at all.

In hard times, we can read this verse as "God is near." We cannot live on a sunny mountaintop every day. There are shadowed valleys in our sin-wracked world, but God is near and attentive to you and your prayers. He offers protection, guidance, and refuge to those who seek him. God's outcome may not appear as you thought it would, but we can trust his near and gracious sovereignty in every situation.

Thank you for your nearness, God. When I'm in trouble, I know you will answer my call with love and mercy. Give me the confidence to follow your guiding Holy Spirit.

IN AND OUT

Brothers and sisters, think about the things that are good and worthy of praise. Think about the things that are true and honorable and right and pure and beautiful and respected. Do what you learned and received from me, what I told you, and what you saw me do. And the God who gives peace will be with you.

PHILIPPIANS 4:8-9 NCV

Have you ever eaten the wrong snack right before bed, making you toss and turn all night? That snack that you thought would be so satisfying ended up leaving you restless and miserable.

What we put in our minds will come out, affecting our peace. How can we ask God for peace when we keep putting garbage in our minds? If your life is full of anxiety, check what you are feeding your mind. Is it junk on television or social media? Garbage in magazines or friends' conversations? Even the news can be garbage in our ears if it creates more fear than education!

God gives peace when we ask for it, but we must also diligently guard our hearts and minds from things that are not true, honorable, righteous, innocent, beautiful, and respectable.

God, I repent of the garbage I pile up in my soul. Thank you for your Word, which shows me where true peace comes from. Create in me a clean heart, oh God.

CREATIVE GIFTS

He has filled him with the Spirit of God, with wisdom, with understanding, with knowledge and with all kinds of skills—to make artistic designs for work in gold, silver and bronze.

EXODUS 35:31-32 NLT

Creative souls, God is calling you. You may think you have no worth in the kingdom because your skill lies with paper, cloth, or clay, but God has written down your name and purpose. You may find yourself lost in a sea of teachers and preachers, whose gifts are equally important, if you are in those categories, but your creative gifts are not forgotten. Your skills are from the Holy Spirit, and they are worthy and useful in the body of Christ. God sees your paint-splattered hands and messy desk, and he smiles. He has a plan and a purpose for your work!

Obedience is recognizing who we were created to be and living it. Don't fight against how God made you. Instead, ask the Holy Spirit to fill your art, move your hands, and bring God glory through your work. Ask God to show you how your craft can be used to bring others into his kingdom.

God is crying out to his creative children's hearts. Your creativity is deeply desired and needed in the kingdom of heaven.

God, I bring you every gift I have, even the less traditional ones I thought were useless. Use me! You are the potter; I am the clay.

GENIE IN A BOTTLE

*"Did I not tell you that if you believed,
you would see the glory of God?"*

JOHN 11:40 NRSV

Wouldn't it be nice if God showed up on our timetable?
If we are honest, sometimes we want God to act like a magic
genie, granting our wishes exactly when we want them. In
John 11, Mary and Martha might have wanted the same.
When they sent a message to Jesus that their brother, Lazarus,
was ill, they wanted him to drop everything to come and heal
him. They fully believed Jesus could heal him.

Still, Jesus didn't come. He didn't act like a genie, and
Lazarus died. Mary and Martha were distraught and confused.
The healing they had believed in so strongly had not come.
Instead, Jesus performed a miracle that would create and
strengthen faith in him, a miracle that would bring God the
most glory. It was not healing, but resurrection. God may have
seemed late to Mary and Martha, but he was right on time.

You may be asking God why he isn't healing a relationship,
sickness, or tense situation. Maybe he is looking for
resurrection, waiting to bring God the most glory. Pray for the
same! God wants to do something even better in your life. Do
you trust him and his timing?

**God, I often do not understand your will and timetable.
Help me to remain steadfast in faith, with my eyes on you
and my will aligned with yours.**

REDEEMING LOVE

God is love.

1 JOHN 4:8 NLT

Tolerance is the motto of the day, yet one of the most intolerant acts in the world happened on a cross two thousand years ago. A man who had done no wrong was beaten, nailed to a cross, and murdered for the guilt of the whole world, and God let it happen. In fact, he orchestrated it. God doesn't seem very tolerant of evil, does he? The cross sums up the character of God, marrying his love and mercy with his justice and holiness. Our God will not tolerate us, but he does love us with a perfect, redeeming love.

Jesus never affirmed everyone he encountered as right. He never told the women at the well that it was totally cool that she had four husbands and now a lover. He pointed out sins. He didn't want to tolerate people; he wanted to love them. Jesus called for right and wrong, and he would be called intolerant in today's society because he did so.

As you go into the workforce and the larger world, you are going to encounter many people living dead in their sin. The world is going to scream at you to tolerate them. The challenge is do more than tolerate; it's to love, as God loved us.

God, let me hold firm to the truth of Scripture. Thank you for loving me, not tolerating me. That love brought me from darkness into glorious light. Help me to love others the way you love me.

MAY

We know that all things
work together for good
to those who love God,
to those who are the called
according to His purpose.

ROMANS 8:28 NKJV

GOD IS GREATER

"If you sinful people know how to give good gifts to your children, how much more will your heavenly Father give good gifts to those who ask him."

MATTHEW 7:11 NLT

There once was a judge who didn't give a rip about anyone or anything. There was also a widow who kept coming to him asking for justice. Finally, the judge got annoyed and gave her what she wanted.

There also was a friend who went to his neighbor to borrow some bread, since his out-of-town friends had arrived in the middle of the night. The neighbor pretended he couldn't hear him at the door, but the friend was persistent. He knew that cultural obligation bound his neighbor to help. Finally, he received what he needed.

You may have read these parables before in Luke. Do you catch the irony of what Jesus is saying? God, defender of the widows (Ps. 68:5), would never act like the judge; he is the better opposite! As a neighbor, God watches over us, always willing to answer the door (Ps. 121:4). In today's verse, even we, as wicked human beings, give gifts. How can we not be confident that he will respond in love when we pray? Be bold and persistent in your prayers.

God, you are a good father with good gifts, the defender of the orphan and the widow. You are the one who never sleeps and is always near. Let me know your true character and seek you boldly!

REUNIONS

As for me, how good it is to be near God!
PSALM 73:28 NLT

Graduation can send you into a new season of long distance relationships. Although the distance is hard and you fiercely miss your friends, it is extra meaningful when you do see them again, and extra sweet to be near that friend who just gets you. Thinking about your reunion makes the distance less painful.

Reunions are a good analogy of today's verse and how we feel when united with God. It is good, comforting, and so sweet to be near to God, the one who created us, knows us inside and out, fights for us, and listens to us. God is love, and he loves us so deeply. To be near to him is pure goodness!

Although you have to wait to experience this joy with your friends, God is always near. He never pulls away. He is the same yesterday, today, and forever. We are the ones who push him away and separate ourselves from him. Draw near, and let nothing hinder you! On the Last Day, you will see him face-to-face at the greatest reunion of all.

Draw me near to you, God. Let me come into your courts with praise. Thank you for never changing or moving away. I love you with all my being!

HOW MANY DAYS?

Teach us to number our days
that we may get a heart of wisdom.

PSALM 90:12 ESV

When you are young, aging seems like...well that it is ages away! Rationally, you realize that you will age someday, but that almost seems like an abstract concept. Because of this, it is easy to buy into the message of YOLO. You feel the liberty to make terribly unwise decisions because you reason that at some point, when you are older, you will fix any mistakes you made in your youth.

The truth is you have no idea how long you have on this earth. "Numbering your days" is an expression that means you choose wisely what you do every day because you aren't guaranteed the next. There is great wisdom in striving to live each and every day with purpose. Let the Lord use your days to bring him glory.

Father, I pray that I would be wise beyond my years. Help me live with purpose and intention now and not assume that I will be able to later. Help me gain a heart of wisdom in my youth.

TOUGH CHOICES

"No one takes it from me, but I lay it down of my own accord. I have authority to lay it down, and I have authority to take it up again. This charge I have received from my Father."

JOHN 10:8 ESV

Should I paint my nails Perfectly Pink or Metallic Shimmer? Should I get an iPhone or a Samsung Galaxy? Should I apply to that college or this one? Or to both? We all have tough choices to make, but let's face it. Most of them are pretty easy compared to the choice that Jesus made. Jesus, the Son of God, *chose* to humble himself and become a baby born in a stable. Jesus *chose* to work in a carpenter shop alongside his dad. Jesus *chose* to die on the cross. All he had to do was call out, and thousands of angels would have come instantly. But he didn't. He *chose* to lay down his life. Why? Because he loved the world—he loved you.

The only way it was possible for you to have a relationship with a holy, perfect God was for your sins to be forgiven and taken away. And that could only happen through sacrifice and the blood that Jesus shed. He knew that only through his death could you have life. So, next time you're faced with a tough choice, remember the one who loved you and made a huge choice for your good.

Thank you, Jesus, for willingly laying your life down for me. I am so grateful for your sacrifice. Help me love you in return.

NOT JUST A CHILDREN'S SONG

Jesus loves me this I know,
For the Bible tells me so.
Little ones to him belong;
They are weak, but he is strong.

It's probably the most popular Sunday school song. Church children grow up hearing it almost from birth. And those who have never attended church also seem to be familiar with it. It's a simple song but absolutely foundational to our faith.

You are loved. The Bible illustrates that better than any other book. It reveals God's plan for redeeming the earth through Jesus. He goes to extravagant lengths to save us and win our hearts. Read your Bible. It will remind you of God's love when you feel unworthy, alone, or when your heart is tempted to look elsewhere for love and acceptance.

Father, thank you for your love demonstrated in your Word. Draw me to your Word and reveal your love to me again.

THE PRE-EXISTENT JESUS

In the beginning was the Word, and the Word was with
God and the Word was God. He was with God in the
beginning. Through him all things were made; without him
nothing was made that has been made.

JOHN 1:1-3 NIV

God the Father wasn't the only one present when the earth was created. There were two others there as well: the Holy Spirit and Jesus. It's a beautiful picture that we won't fully grasp this side of eternity. But God exists in three separate persons, and those three expressions of God have existed from before there was time.

Jesus' existence didn't begin the day he was placed in Mary's womb. He has always been and will always be. He is the beginning and the end. Sometimes it's hard to grasp what God might actually be like because he is so different from us. When you wrestle with that, just look to Jesus. He is the exact representation of God (Hebrews 1:3). If you want to know how God acts, feels, and responds to his children, then study the actions, tears, and words of Jesus.

Jesus, thank you that you have always been there and will always be there. I trust you. Please reveal the Father to me that I might adore you more.

A GOOD LEADER

"I am the good shepherd. The good shepherd lays down his life for the sheep."

JOHN 10:11 NIV

What do you look for in a leader? If we are to bring others into a relationship with Christ, we are all called to become leaders ourselves. One of the best examples we could ever ask for in leadership was Jesus himself. And he called himself a good shepherd. There was good reason for this. Though a shepherd, at the time, was not a job that many aspired to, it called for special skills. A shepherd had to guide his flock of sheep without scaring them into submission. Sheep are known to make poor choices when operating under fear.

Shepherds needed to nourish, comfort, lead, correct, and protect their sheep. And most importantly, a good shepherd would encourage those in their care to follow his example and stay with him. Are you a leader for Christ's kingdom? Are you encouraging others to follow your example, comforting them in times of need and correcting them gently when the situation calls for it?

Lord, please help me to display good leadership in my life. I want to model myself after you, the good shepherd, and care for others by leading them to you.

A MARATHON LIFE

We are surrounded by a great cloud of people whose lives tell us what faith means. So let us run the race that is before us and never give up.

HEBREWS 12:1 NCV

If you are an athlete, then you know what it means to persevere. Pushing yourself past your wall, breaking down what you thought were your limits, and hanging on to the end are all a part of an athlete's way of life.

Our lives as Christians are like a marathon. There is the world's greatest prize waiting for us if we can push through and endure until the end. When we cross the finish line, we get to run into the arms of Jesus. Hardship will come, but we can get through it if we just keep our eyes on that prize.

Lord, help me keep my eyes on the prize—eternal life with you. Help me through the tough times and give me the ability to persevere. I know the prize waiting at the end is worth it!

DWELLING ON TRUTH

Listen, my dearest darling,
You are so beautiful—
You are beauty itself to me!

SONG OF SONGS 4:7 TPT

Do you ever hear voices in your head that tell you you're not good enough? Do you need others' approval and opinions to give you confidence? There is good news: you are enough! God made you just the way he wants you. Those voices in your head that say you're not good enough are lies.

You can do anything God calls you to. When the voice of discouragement comes, silence it. When you find yourself desiring approval, shift your thinking and seek God for confidence. What God thinks of you matters the most.

God, the more I practice dwelling on the truth, the more I will see how valuable I am in your eyes. I want you to define me and be proud of who that is.

SHELTERING PROMISES

Truly he is my rock and my salvation;
he is my fortress, I will never be shaken.

PSALM 62:2 NIV

Life is always changing, whether we like it or not. Sometimes, it changes and moves faster than we anticipated. Changes can bring blessings and joy, uncertainty and fear. In response, we cling to anything that will make us feel safe, comforted, and secure.

During times of change or transition, we can always cling to God. He is unchanging, and so are his promises. His character doesn't waver. We can find comfort and security in him, knowing that no matter how the world around us evolves he stays the same.

With that trust, we can lean into him during every step of our life. We can draw strength from him when life is chaotic and unsettling. As the world spins and spins, he grounds and stabilizes our hearts. He offers protection that the world cannot. He promises to cover us when we need covering. Take refuge in these promises.

God, I can handle whatever change comes my way, knowing I can find stability and safety in you. I am grateful for your unchanging and unwavering help in time of need. Reassure me of your promises today.

ASK WITH CONFIDENCE

Let us then approach God's throne of grace with
confidence, so that we may receive mercy and find grace
to help us in our time of need.

HEBREWS 4:16 NIV

Asking for help isn't always easy. The thought can make our skin go cold and our pulses quicken. It makes us nervous. Sometimes, our pride interferes. We don't want to be seen as weak or needy. More often than not, we are fearful of rejection. Perhaps our needs are too little or unimportant. These fears might stem from times we have been ridiculed or rejected by others. The sting of rejection can smart for a long time, convincing us that we are foolish to ask for help.

Instead, we let our needs go unasked. We struggle alone. Our pride gets in the way of the support we need. We can always go to God with every need, big or small. He won't reject us or turn us away, because we are important to him. He loves to hear from us and help us. He loves it when we run to him, and he will warmly embrace us. He will give us grace. He loves us through our weakness, our needs, and our mistakes. He is God, and we are his.

We can approach God without fear, again and again.

Lord, thank you for your grace and mercy. I desperately need it! Wrap me in your arms today, and remind me of your constant love and support.

VULNERABILITY

The temptations in your life are no different from what others experience. And God is faithful. He will not allow the temptation to be more than you can stand. When you are tempted, he will show you a way out so that you can endure.

1 CORINTHIANS 10:13 NLT

Struggling with temptations is exhausting. Struggling with temptations alone? Even worse. Satan wants us to believe that we are battling by ourselves. He loves it when we feel overwhelmed by and ashamed of the challenges of walking a life with God. He wants us to hide our battle scars in shame, isolated from other believers. The more alone we feel, the weaker we are, and the more likely we are to give in to our temptations.

Don't listen! Vulnerability is beautiful. In vulnerability, we discover that we aren't alone in our struggles with temptation. Every single believer struggles with temptations. Vulnerability ushers in encouragement and love, empowering us to conquer whatever we face. Vulnerability brings strength, not weakness.

We can tell others our temptations and not be ashamed. We can reach out to God, and he will give us a way out. We don't have to hide or battle without help. God gives us the strength and victory of his right hand.

Lord God, even though I am tempted, I don't ever have to feel abandoned or alone. Thank you for your strength in my vulnerability. Help me to embrace it and welcome helpers into my life. Thank you for this life of freedom.

WHERE IS HOME?

"Have I not commanded you? Be strong and courageous. Do not be afraid; do not be discouraged, for the Lord your God will be with you wherever you go."

JOSHUA 1:9 NASB

Sometimes, the most challenging step in following our dreams is the very first step outside our comfort zone, into the unknown. Home represents safety, love, acceptance, and comfort. Home is where our family and friends are. The door is always open, ready to usher us into the warmth.

Leaving all that good behind is scary, especially if it our first time digging up our roots to plant them in a new place. It doesn't matter where we take our feet, hearts, and luggage, because we are never alone in an unfamiliar place.

God promises to be with us every step of the way. In him, no matter what adventure we take or journey we find ourselves on, we are safe, loved, accepted, and comforted. He is the reason we can take that first step. Since he is our home, we can be brave wherever we go.

Jesus, thank you for being my home. Thank you for the courage and comfort of knowing that you are always with me. Remind me of your presence, and help me step out bravely.

LEAVE THE CHAINS BEHIND

*It is for freedom that Christ has set us free. Stand firm,
then, and do not let yourselves be burdened again by a
yoke of slavery.*

GALATIANS 5:1 NIV

What value does freedom have if it's refused? A prisoner
can be offered freedom, but unless he allows the handcuffs to
be removed and unless he lets someone lead him out from the
bars, he will never be free. He will always be a prisoner.

How often to we stay in a cell of captivity by our own
choosing? How often do we reject freedom that was freely
given to us?

Freedom is worthless if we don't grasp it. It means boldly
refusing whatever lifestyle or sin entangled us in the past. It
means rejecting lies that bind us back into our chains. God
gave us freedom from sin as a gift meant to be embraced and
enjoyed, but we can choose to reject his gift of freedom. We can
chose day-by-day to live as a prisoner, or Jesus can set us free.

**God, help me accept your gift of freedom today and every
day. Thank you that I can live a full and joyful life without
being bound and tied to my past.**

WALLS OF REJECTION

*"All that the Father gives me will come to me,
and whoever comes to me I will never cast out."*

JOHN 6:37 ESV

At some point, all of us experience the pain of rejection. To be turned away or told that we are worthless is damaging and disorienting. It can leave us raw and cynical.

Many of the walls we build in our hearts have their foundation in past hurt. We begin to believe that if we don't let others in, we reduce the risk of hurt. Why have a relationship if it could mean rejection and pain?

Our walls can't exist in a relationship with God because we cannot hide anything from him. He has no walls, and he always welcomes us into his presence. He desires a deep relationship with us. We don't have to be standoffish because there is no reason to guard ourselves from perfect, unconditional love. We don't have to protect ourselves from him because he is our protection. No matter who we are, he will never reject us.

Jesus, help me trust your love. Fear of rejection keeps me behind walls, but I know that you can tear down all barriers. Let me live a rich and full life in you.

145

RUN DOWN

"Come to me, all you who are weary and burdened, and I will give you rest."

MATTHEW 11:28 NIV

How often do we run ourselves ragged? We add more and more to our schedules and social life. Saying no is a foreign concept. We measure our success by our accomplishments, so we push ourselves to do more and to be more. We don't slow down until our bodies and minds force us to, so sick and weary that we shut down.

We strive and strive until we reach the end of our rope weak, broken, and sick. Even our best intentions to follow God fall short if we aren't getting life from the one who loves us.

There is rest in Jesus. When we are weary and overwhelmed by life's unending demands, he wants us to go to him, be it a run, walk, or crawl. Without him, we will make ourselves sick and tired. He longs to be our place of rest. He desires to refresh and restore us. We simply have to leave the demands of the world behind and go to him.

God, help me slow down. I need you to drown out the noise and chaos of the everyday. I am so grateful that you provide me with a place to sit in the quiet, to feel loved and encouraged. Let me pause. Let me rest.

IT'S CASUAL

Run from sexual sin! No other sin so clearly affects the body as this one does. For sexual immorality is a sin against your own body. Don't you realize that your body is the temple of the Holy Spirit, who lives in you and was given to you by God? You do not belong to yourself, for God bought you with a high price. So you must honor God with your body.

1 Corinthians 6:18-20 NLT

Sex. No big deal, right? Movies, TV shows, billboards, and magazines—all these portray sex casually and flippantly. Subtle messages reach us this way, whispering that it's okay to have what we want when we want it. Modesty and abstinence have no worth. Surrounded by these messages, it is easy to get caught up in our sex-obsessed world, desensitized to what we see and participate in.

God wants us to protect and value our sexuality. He cherishes our hearts and bodies and wants to keep us from harm, not fun. Sex was created to be sacred, honored, and protected in marriage. It is a gift between spouses, not a commodity.

Sex is a big deal! It is a wonderful creation from God. Sex outside of marriage exposes us to a world of pain, and it can leave us feeling empty and used. Our loving God wants us to wait until the time is right, and then we can enjoy it completely.

God, you value purity because you value my heart. Thank you for seeing me as someone worth protecting and cherishing. Give me the strength to wait and to value myself the way you value me.

CHILDLIKE DREAMING

There is no fear in love; but perfect love casts out fear,
because fear involves punishment, and the one who fears is
not perfected in love.

1 JOHN 4:18 NASB

When we were little, dreams were always within reach. We could do anything we wanted to do and be whoever we wanted to be. We had faith that we could change the word for the better and make a positive mark in people's lives.

As we grew up, doubt and fear crept in. Maybe we weren't meant for greatness, and only a few were chosen to do amazing things for God. Perhaps we weren't good enough in God's eyes to be chosen. We bought into that fear and let childhood dreams trickle out of our fingertips. Doubt made us settle for less than what God desired for us. We lost faith in ourselves because we couldn't imagine that what God had planned for us.

With childlike faith, we can trust God with our future. He loves us so much, and there is no dream from God that we can't obtain. We can set our eyes on Him, confident that he has good in store for us.

God, I am so tempted to allow fear of the future to steal away your dreams for me. Help me to cling tightly to your love and those dreams. Let my confidence in you propel me to everything you have in store for me.

TRUE SECURITY

The Lord is my strength and my defense;
he has become my salvation.
He is my God, and I will praise him,
my father's God, and I will exalt him.

EXODUS 15:2 NIV

Most of us desperately try to secure our futures. We focus on keeping our lives in order. We depend on a professional degree, finances, our health, or our relationships. If we have the right career, we think our future is secure. If we are in control of our finances, then nothing can harm us; if we work out every day and eat right, we'll have perfect health; and if we marry and have children, then we will never be alone.

These are false sources of security. We only feel safe when life is going as we planned. But the job market could fail, and we could find ourselves in financial crisis or facing a grim health diagnosis, and our relationships can dissolve.

The only secure thing promised is Jesus. He is our safety when the world crumbles around us. He is our strength when we are weak and defenseless. We can praise him even when life is uncertain and messy. When everything falls away, he remains.

Jesus, let my security rest in you and not on what's around me. Thank you for being my safety in a world that isn't stable. May my focus be on you, not my earthly comforts.

EMPTY FRIDGES

"Don't worry about these things, saying, 'What will we eat? What will we drink? What will we wear?' These things dominate the thoughts of unbelievers, but your heavenly Father already knows all your needs."

MATTHEW 6:31-32 NLT

Have you lain awake at night, paralyzed with worry over your finances and future? When the fridge is bare, your bank account is dangerously low, and your paycheck barely covers the month's bills, it's hard to stay calm. Worry and fear can make us emotionally, physically, and spiritually sick. It is a terrible way to live, and not the way God wants his children to live.

God sees all of our needs, large and small. Even if the numbers don't add up, we can sleep well when we put our trust and hope in the God that feeds, clothes, and shelters us. We can have peace in any situation, knowing that the God who loves us will take care of us. He commands us to stop worrying and leave all the details to him.

God is the best father, and he provides more than we ever will need. Because of his promised provision, worry has no place in our lives. He will carry us.

God, thank you for being a good father. Let my trust in you conquer my fears. Let my focus not be on my worries and the cares of this world, which will never disappear, but on your great love instead.

DID YOU HEAR ABOUT . . .

A perverse person stirs up conflict,
and a gossip separates close friends.

PROVERBS 16:28 NIV

Have you ever felt yucky from a conversation you had about another person? In the moment, it may be entertaining to let our words fly without much thought, but our words are powerful. Beautiful or ugly, words can give life or destroy it.

It may seem harmless to engage in a conversation about another person. However, gossip can destroy friendships and damage the person on the receiving end of the gossip.

It's good to stop and think before we engage in conversation. Is the topic of the conversation not only truthful but also loving and encouraging? If not, then we are responsible for changing the subject. God wants us to love one another deeply with both actions and words. We can show others love and grace by refusing to talk behind their backs. We can be trustworthy by keeping unkind thoughts and opinions to ourselves.

God help me to be wise with my words. I want to be a friend that loves, uplifts, and encourages, someone for others to trust and lean on. Open my eyes to gossip I may not always notice.

SUIT UP

Stand firm then, with the belt of truth buckled around your waist, with the breastplate of righteousness in place, and with your feet fitted with the readiness that comes from the gospel of peace. In addition to all this, take up the shield of faith, with which you can extinguish all the flaming arrows of the evil one. Take the helmet of salvation and the sword of the Spirit, which is the word of God.

EPHESIANS 6:14-17 NIV

Following Jesus often times means going against the grain of the world. We don't usually like to stand out among our peers, but blending in may compromise our values and beliefs.

If we push back against cultural norms, we may experience harsh criticism from others who don't understand or agree with us. We might be disliked, misunderstood, or even shunned. Under pressure, it's tempting to give in to what others want and expect of us.

We don't have to be afraid during those times because God has given us the tools we need to be strong. We are made righteous through him through the faith he gave us. He has given us his true Word. And we are not empty-handed, so we can stay strong even when we feel weak. We can bravely stand up for what is right and true, clad in his armor.

Thank you, Jesus, for preparing me to courageously live for you. I am so thankful that you haven't left me to battle alone or unarmed. Thank you for your strengthening Word. Nurture my faith, so that I can be strong for you.

PERMANENCE

What we suffer now is nothing compared to the glory he will reveal to us later.

ROMANS 8:18 NLT

We are not strangers to pain, loss, grief, or struggle. Sometimes, life is chock-full of these things. Our attempt to understand why can result in more pain and confusion. Why are we struggling? Why is this person or situation so hurtful and broken? We all want to find purpose in our struggles, hoping that it will alleviate some pain. No matter how we try, we may never find purpose in it.

We can know two things for certain. One, God loves us through every trial and circumstance. He feels our pain, and he grieves and mourns with us. Two, all our struggles pale in comparison to the joy that comes from God.

Pain and struggle is temporary; the love and joy from Jesus is permanent. It will never be taken from us. We can draw strength from that promise.

Jesus, thank you for your strong presence in my life. Please comfort me in my struggles, and remind me that I am not alone in my pain. Open my eyes to your good influence, even when life is difficult. Thank you for your promises, which sustain me through my hardships. I am thankful for your love.

WAITING, WAITING

Be strong, and let your heart take courage,
all you who wait for the Lord.

PSALM 31:24 NRSV

Waiting feels like a waste of time. It can make us frustrated, annoyed, and anxious, and these feelings tend to get worse the longer we have to wait, especially when there is no end in sight. But what if waiting has a purpose? What if we learned to love waiting? What if a wait is actually beauty in disguise?

Waiting on God is a blessing. It makes us stop what we are doing and set our eyes on Jesus. It forces us to rely on him alone. It persuades us to relinquish control and put our trust in Him. Ultimately, it strengthens our faith and draws us closer to him.

There are so many opportunities to wait on God in this life. Instead of getting frustrated, we can choose to embrace the wait, being thankful for everything God has for us in it. Waiting on God is gift.

God, when I am waiting on you, help me quiet my anxious and hurried heart. Teach me to draw closer to you, and fill my heart with ever-growing patience.

THE GRAND PLAN

What does the Lord require of you? To act justly and to love mercy and to walk humbly with your God.

MICAH 6:8 NIV

How often do we complicate what God requires of us? We spend money on self-help books and gift tests, as if they will reveal his ultimate plan for us. We concentrate our energies on discovering his mysterious and great purpose for our lives. Worry makes us sick. What if the steps in life we are taking are the wrong ones? What if we aren't paying close enough attention? We may blow it and completely miss our chance to please him.

We don't have to stress. God's expectations for his children are simple and clearly laid out, with no secret steps or hidden clues. We can live in his will by walking with him. We can give grace and mercy to everyone we encounter, and we can be fair in our actions and decisions.

If we set our hearts to do these things, then we are fulfilling what he wants of us. There is no grand plan, and we are not missing out. We simply need to be humble, fair, and gracious.

Thank you, God, that your desires for my life are not complicated or unattainable. Help me to be humble, fair, and gracious every day. My desire is to please you and love you. May living for you bring joy and satisfaction to my life.

LISTEN FOR THE TRUTH

You are altogether beautiful, my darling,
beautiful in every way.

SONG OF SOLOMON 4:7 NLT

Thanks to today's social media, the game of comparison is too easy: *You aren't good enough; You're ugly; He's smarter than you; She's more successful.* We look at the person next to us or on our screen. Seeing their attractiveness and success, we wonder why their life is so perfect and flawless when ours feels like such a mess. We let these lies lessen our self worth and perception of ourselves.

The truth is that we all carry insecurities and struggles, even those people who seem to have their lives in order. The other truth is that God loves you for you. He doesn't see our brokenness and mess. He only sees the beauty we all posses, beauty that he himself gave us.

Whenever we are bombarded with demeaning lies, we can combat them with God's loving truth. He sees us in a light that the world doesn't see, and he says: "You are good enough; you are beautiful; you are smart; and you are worthy, loved, and irreplaceable."

God, I sometimes struggle to see the beauty that you created in me. Open my eyes to the deep love you have for me, Lord. Let your truth wash away all of my doubts and insecurities, and let me see myself and others as you do.

LET HIM SHINE

The Holy Spirit produces this kind of fruit in our lives:
love, joy, peace, patience, kindness, goodness,
faithfulness, gentleness, and self-control.

GALATIANS 5:22, 23 NLT

As Christians, we want Christ to shine through us. We long to be more patient, loving, kind, joyful, generous, and faithful, filled with grace and forgiveness. However, when we look deep into our hearts and analyze ourselves, we discover things that don't line up with Christ.

We might expect instantaneous change, and when it doesn't happen, we become discouraged and frustrated. We work harder, determined to be better. That tactic seems to work, until we find ourselves again sunk in old sins and patterns. It becomes an unending cycle: sin, discouragement, determination, and sin again.

We forget that we can't work this great change alone. We need the Holy Spirit to gently teach and mold our hearts. Even if we aren't seeing instant progress, we can be confident that he is working in our lives. When we submit our lives to him, humble about our failures, he will continue to lovingly and graciously work. Jesus can shine through our weaknesses and imperfections.

Lord God, thank you for the work you are doing in my life. Thank you for taking this hardened heart and shaping it to be more like you. Help me to see the internal work and fruits you are producing in my life.

OUR GREATEST FRIEND

Cast your cares on the Lord and he will sustain you;
he will never let the righteous be shaken.

PSALM 55:22 NIV

At the end of a long and difficult day, sometimes all we want to do is crash on the couch, wrap up in blankets, and call a good friend to vent or cry. That friend won't judge or criticize us. He or she cares and understands. Sharing our difficulties with a friend can lightens our burdens and lifts our spirits. We find comfort in knowing that, no matter what we are going through, we aren't alone.

Jesus is our friend, too, and he wants us to share our troubles with him. He responds with nothing but love, encouragement, and understanding. His everyday presence in our lives carries us through our struggles. We can trust him to be there for us because he genuinely cares about us and our lives. He is our perfect best friend.

If a day is extra long and life seems extra difficult, we can talk to him. Our cares don't annoy him. He wants to walk with us through both good and bad times. With him, a bad day is just that—a bad day. It won't destroy us.

Jesus, thank you for your listening ear. Sometimes, life is overwhelming, and having you as a friend makes tough times more bearable. I am grateful for your unending friendship.

LET GO

"I will never again remember their sins and lawless deeds."
HEBREWS 10:17 TLB

Ever tried to make a fresh start, but shame held you back? Shame is powerful. We all carry regretful or embarrassing memories and decisions. They are hard to shake off, even if they make us feel terrible. Maybe we hold on because we feel unworthy of forgiveness, or maybe we want to continue paying penance for our crimes, wrongly believing that it will make us feel better. We hide, guilty and ashamed.

Shame separates us from God's freedom and grace. It keeps us from the very God who has already forgiven and forgotten our sins. Our shame can dig so deep that we can't run into the arms of God, but that is exactly what he wants us to do. He wants us to let go of our pasts, our regrets, and our shame, embracing his grace and forgiveness.

Jesus carried our shame and destroyed it on the cross. We don't have to bear it. We live in freedom, not defined by a long list of sins. There is no record of wrongs, only acceptance and forgiveness. We can come out of hiding to a God who loves us freely.

Thank you, Jesus, for giving me a free and full life. Thank you for your grace, which draws me to you. I am so thankful that I don't have to hide from my past sins or be defined by them. I lay my shame at your feet; help me fully experience your love.

159

KINGLY FRIENDSHIP

"I do not call you servants any longer, because the servant does not know what the master is doing; but I have called you friends, because I have made known to you everything that I have heard from my Father."

JOHN 15:15 NRSV

Sometimes, we picture God as this distant, commanding power that we need to be wary of and obey. He is all-powerful; he is God. How wonderful is it that our walk with God also gives us precious friendship with him?

He isn't distant and unreachable. We can spend every moment of every day with him. We speak to him, share our hearts with him, cry with him, and rejoice with him. In turn, he shares his heart and thoughts with us. He ushers us into a deep and intimate relationship with him. He doesn't use his power to control us; instead, he shows us perfect love and friendship. He leads us with a gentle and loving hand, not a fist.

The King of the world longs for a deep relationship with us. He doesn't hide from us. He is close. He is true. He is reachable.

Thank you, God, for your friendship. I am so thankful that your presence in my life is constant. I am so blessed to walk this life with you. Help me to seek you as you seek me.

GOD IS BIGGER

"You of little faith, why are you so afraid?" Then he got up and rebuked the winds and the waves, and it was completely calm.

MATTHEW 8:26 NIV

One of the biggest obstacles in following God is fear. We let our doubts and fears overshadow God's call because we are looking at the situation through our weak eyes, forgetting to put God in the equation. We forget that he is omniscient and all-powerful. We minimize his power and position in the world.

We obsess about the what-ifs. What if we fail? What if we are mocked and scorned? What if we lose everything? Our insecurities take over, and they refuse to let us move in God's direction.

God is bigger than all our what-ifs. If he has called us to do something, he won't let us fail. He will walk with us every step of the way, calming the noise and chaos around us. We only need faith in him, faith that he is stronger than our fears, doubts, and weaknesses. No matter what situation we might be facing, he is the king.

God, my life belongs to you. My faith is small, but I know that you will conquer all of my fears. I am thankful that the trouble in this world is nothing compared to your power and strength. When I am hesitant and afraid, please share your peace with me.

JUNE

Be my rock of refuge,
to which I can always go;
give the command to save me,
for you are my rock
and my fortress....
You have been my hope,
Sovereign Lord,
my confidence since my youth.

PSALM 71:3, 5 NIV

PRIDE AND CONFIDENCE

Clothe yourselves with humility toward one another, because,
"God opposes the proud but shows favor to the humble."

1 PETER 5:5 NIV

Sometimes, we confuse pride and confidence. Confidence in God is a wonderful thing. Pride can be ugly and destructive. It can separate us from those who love us and keep us from living a rich and grace-filled life with God. It allows us to get caught up in our achievements. It blinds us to the brokenhearted and hurting around us.

If we don't guard ourselves, pride can trick us into believing that we are better than others, especially those different than us. This can only cause division and hurt. There is no acceptance, growth, or love in pride. It makes us forget that we all are sinners, desperately in need of God's grace and love. Every single person was created to need God. Every one of us is weak and broken.

We need to lay down our attitudes of pride and superiority and learn to live with one another in love. Jesus loves a humble heart. He can forgive our weakness and wash us with grace, but he can't reach a heart hardened with pride.

Empty me of my pride, Jesus, and fill me with humility. Help me love those around me deeply and live in close relationship with you. I need you to continue to humble me so that I can learn and grow. Give me confident faith in you.

SERVING GOD ALONE

*Always work enthusiastically for the Lord, for you know that
nothing you do for the Lord is ever useless.*

1 CORINTHIANS 15:58 NLT

Everyone wants to work for God in big ways. Some
adventurous callings make our hearts quicken in anticipation.
Maybe you want to work overseas with orphans in Africa or
be on the front line of politics. Perhaps preaching as a well-
known and respected Christian leader is a personal dream.
Sometimes, God calls us for tasks that aren't glamorous or
prestigious. They seem tedious and boring. Most times, they
come without reward or social recognition. They are done
secretly and quietly, and no one sees them but God.

Regardless of how we are called to serve God, our
motivation should always be to please him. Serving God
for human praise will always leave us feeling empty and
unfulfilled. If we set our hearts on serving God wholeheartedly,
regardless of the payback, his joy will fill us.

Big or small, every act done in the name of God is important.
He will take our willing hearts and use them for his service.

God, I am grateful for the opportunity to serve you every
day, in ways both large and small. Thank you for using
me for your glory. Help me to serve in your name, without
searching for praise.

WHAT'S GOING ON?

Trust in the Lord with all your heart and lean not on your own understanding; in all your ways submit to him, and he will make your paths straight.

PROVERBS 3:5-6 NIV

Try as we might, there are times in life when we can't make sense of what God is doing. That confusion may produce doubt and fear in our hearts. No matter how hard we seek to understand we just can't. We aren't God. We can't see everything he sees or know all that he knows.

In times of confusion, we should lean on God even more. He will continue to guide us despite our lack of understanding. Our blindness doesn't make God less faithful, less powerful, or less loving.

Our faith in God will see us through every dark and uncertain time. Our lack of understanding can produce greater reliance on him. Only in the darkness do we recognize our great need for him.

Thank you, God, for remaining faithful, loving, and powerful. Sometimes, I struggle to see you moving, and the darkness brings confusion. Still, I trust you. I trust in your love and care for me and your people. Help me rely on you, and grant me your peace.

BREATH OF LIFE

"Do not fear, for I have redeemed you;
I have summoned you by name; you are mine."

Isaiah 43:1 niv

At one point or another in our lives, you lived apart from God. That past may hold actions or decisions that cause regret, shame, and embarrassment. You might wonder if you can move past what you did. Satan wants you to wallow in these feelings. He wants you to fear that you are unchangeable, unlovable, and unforgivable.

God has redeemed you. He breathed new life and meaning into your brokenness. He set you free from your past and called you his own, and you changed. God remade you into something beautiful because he loves you.

In his love, you can lift your head high. Your past has no power, and your life is transformed. You can rest in knowing that God, who knows you completely, calls you his child. What a wonderful feeling, to belong, to be known, to be loved. To be given a new name, and a new identity.

Thank you, Jesus, for loving me enough to redeem my life. I am no longer a slave to my old life and habits. Remind me to live my freedom with joy and praise.

WORD OF TRUTH

Truthful words stand the test of time,
but lies are soon exposed.

PROVERBS 12:19 NLT

Lies are sneaky. They often dress up as truth. They cause conflict, mistrust, and confusion. They have a nasty habit of subtly worming their way into our hearts, minds, and lives. God wants us to hold on to his truth, but how can we decipher truth from clever deceit?

Time is a great revealer of truth. Lies will fall apart and disappear, while truth remains strong and intact. While we wait, we can put our hope and trust in the truth God has already revealed to us in his Word: He is loving; His love always endures; He is unchanging; and He is gracious, compassionate, and always forgiving.

These truths will stand against any lie. His Word is full of life and truth. We can let his truth penetrate our hearts, and we can use it as a shield against any deceit that attempts to take hold of our lives.

God, thank you for your unchanging truth, which brings life, hope, and comfort. I am grateful for your word that is at my fingertips. Remind me to pick up your book every day. Let it pierce my heart and mind, battling any lies I encounter.

WHITE PICKET FENCE

We live by faith, not by sight.

2 CORINTHIANS 5:7 NIV

We like futures that are clearly laid out for us. We find comfort and safety in a well-thought-out and executed plan like this one: Go to college; Graduate; Land a dream job; Get married; Have children; and Live happily ever after.

If only life was that easy! Sometimes, the future does go according to our plans, but more often it does not. Many unknowns await us, and we are forced to walk by faith.

Faith tells us that God cares deeply about our future and us. Faith reminds us that God is in control and purposeful, despite our present circumstances. No matter what hardship we encounter, faith knows that we will face it with God's support. Everything will work out. We can't always see God's plan for our lives, but we can always feel secure when putting our faith in him. He loves us dearly, and his intentions towards us are good.

Jesus, help me walk by faith and not by sight. I want to trust you, regardless of the uncertainties ahead of me. Please let my faith speak loudest, in every situation.

CONTENTMENT LASTS

True godliness with contentment is itself great wealth.

1 TIMOTHY 6:6 NLT

The pursuit of wealth is alive in America. Many salivate over the American Dream and work to achieve it, sometimes at great personal cost. What if we ignored the status quo and pursued contentment as passionately as we pursued wealth? What if our choices were centered around God, not money, status, and material possessions? What if our joy and peace came from God and not from what the world promises us?

Financial wealth does not last, but contentment is a steady wealth. Contentment gives us satisfaction, no matter what our situation. No one can take our contentment away. It can't be lost or destroyed. It is ours if we want it and seek it. Contentment sustains us through difficult relationships, health struggles, and financial strife, and it doesn't cost a dime. It is a gift from God.

As we plan for the future, the world will tell us that we won't be happy without financial wealth. God tells us that we can experience true and deep joy in him, with or without money. May contentment be our life pursuit.

God, I seek your gift of contentment in this life. Help me be joyful regardless of what circumstance I am in, knowing my satisfaction comes from your love.

PURSUIT

They refused to listen; they forgot the miracles you did for them. So they became stubborn and turned against you, choosing a leader to take them back to slavery. But you are a forgiving God. You are kind and full of mercy. You do not become angry quickly, and you have great love. So you did not leave them.

NEHEMIAH 9:17 NCV

Are these whispers familiar? You really blew it this time. Your choices and decisions have led you down a path that there is no coming back from. There is no way God will open his arms up to you again. You are a lost cause. You are not worth loving or saving.

Sometimes we buy into the lie that God's love for us has limits, and he will refuse to open his arms to us if we cross them. But the lie is just that—a lie, meant to isolate us from the God who pursues our hearts, no matter how far we walk away.

God is slow to anger. He is patient while we struggle, fall, and make mistakes. He doesn't abandon us when we are stubborn and difficult. He calmly waits for our hearts to turn to him again. His love for us is so great and vast that he will never leave us. He is kind when we don't deserve it, and he rains mercy on us when we desperately need it.

Jesus, many times I have walked away from you, but you never leave me. Your love for me is overwhelming, the worth you give me astounding. Thank you for your relentless pursuit and unending patience. Forgive my stubbornness, and help me walk with you.

FINDING FRIENDS

Two people are better off than one, for they can help each other succeed. If one person falls, the other can reach out and help. But someone who falls alone is in real trouble.

ECCLESIASTES 4:9-10 NLT

If you have lived without community, you know what it feels like to be alone. We all want to feel included and wanted. Life transitions often mean leaving family, community, and familiarity behind as we take the next step.

Finding footing on new ground can be lonely. Even the most introverted of us were designed to live in close relationships with others. It can be hard to be vulnerable and initiate new relationships, but the reward is well worth the struggle.

Friends are a treasure. They lift us up when we fall, encouraging us when we are overwhelmed and discouraged. They inspire us to be the best versions of ourselves. They bring joy and fun. They listen, they understand, and they cry with us. With them, we are not alone. In any season of life, if we ask God to bring people into our lives to walk with us, he will. He is the creator of friendships. He loves you, and he doesn't want you to be lonely.

Jesus, sometimes I feel lonely, and I long for close, real friendships. Please bring people into my life to walk and celebrate with, to love and encourage. Thank you for friendship and community.

FULL PLATES

Serve one another humbly in love.

GALATIANS 5:13 NIV

With everything on our plates, the last thing we want to do is add more. However, when we look outside our little worlds, and ourselves, we see people who are desperate for friendship, encouragement, and care all around us. All of us can find people who are hurting and need love.

God wants us to serve others. It doesn't always have to be done in huge, grand gestures. Sometimes, the smallest acts of kindness have the biggest impact. Send an encouraging note to a friend who needs it. Make a meal for an overwhelmed mom. Go visit an older neighbor for a few minutes. Offer to babysit for a couple with young children, so they can have some time together. All these little gifts go a long way in making another person feel valued and loved.

We have the ability to show God's love in everyday moments. We have the opportunity to bless one another in huge ways. They don't require anything but a willing heart and a little bit of your time.

Jesus, thank you for the blessings you have heaped on my plate. Open my eyes to the opportunities in the broken and hurting around me. I desire to love deeply and serve wholeheartedly in your name.

PUT ON GRACE

*With all humility and gentleness, with patience,
bearing with one another in love.*

EPHESIANS 4:2 ESV

We are human. All of us have varying personalities and opinions, and often those differences clash. All of us can think of one friend who gets under our skin, a family member who is hard to love, or a boss who is difficult to work for.

Despite our irritation, we are called to have an attitude of humility, patience, and love for everyone. Jesus' love is for everyone. He doesn't push away any who come to him, freely giving forgiveness and worth. No one is perfect. As broken beings, we make mistakes, and yet God loves us.

If we are struggling to love, we should strip off our frustration and put on grace and acceptance. If we don't, hate can fester inside of us, infecting our souls. When loving is difficult, we need to take a moment to breathe. We can discover lovable attributes in everyone. If we ask God to open our eyes, he will show us how to love that person we find so difficult. He will give us more patience and love than we can hold.

God, show me how to love as you love. Open up my eyes and heart to see clearly those I struggle to love. I want to love deeply, and I want to share grace and acceptance with everyone. Help me put away my annoyances and frustrations, and give me a warm and open heart.

COMMANDER GOD

The Lord will fight for you,
and you shall hold your peace.

EXODUS 14:14 NKJV

Have you ever encountered a battle that you couldn't fight? The problem or enemy was too large, too overwhelming—just too much. Exhausted, we get frustrated by our limited capabilities and discouraged by our lack of control.

Thankfully, we aren't called to fight any battle alone, and some battles aren't ours. There are times when God wants us to be still and wait. He will battle on our behalf. It is hard to do nothing, but the God who fights for us is the same God who quiets storms and moves mountains. We can sit peacefully, knowing that He is strong and victorious. We can celebrate victory before the battle is won.

We serve a God who fights for us. There is peace in knowing that we stand protected behind him as he goes to battle. We can put our weaker weapons down, abandon our fear, and have full confidence in his power, all because of his great love for mercy, justice, and his people.

God, you are victorious! Thank you for being my commander in every battle. When you call me to fight with you, you give me the right weapons. When you ask me to wait, I have peace with you as my shield and protector. Give me keen ears to hear your commands.

TRUE EMPATHY

He was despised and rejected—a man of sorrows,
acquainted with deepest grief.

ISAIAH 53:3 NLT

Our broken hearts crave true empathy and understanding, but often our deepest pains go unspoken. Maybe we feel like no one can understand how we feel. Surely the pain runs too deep for even the closest friend to relate to. Instead of opening up about our feelings, we attempt to bury the hurt. We pretend that everything is okay, when, in truth, we are breaking inside.

It's hard to heal when we hide our wounds. But there is one who will always listen to our cries. He understands what it feels like to be rejected and abused. He has been hurt and alone. He is not a stranger to brokenness and pain.

We find true empathy in Jesus. We can go to him with our deepest wounds and find understanding. He will take away our sorrow, bringing healing to the most broken parts of our lives. Because he loves us, we don't have to hide from Him or pretend that everything is okay. He will hold our hands and walk us through the darkness. He will bring joy in the worst situation. He will not silence our words. He will listen and be our voice when we can't speak.

Jesus, sometimes I feel alone in my grief, but then you remind me of your true empathy. You listen, build me up, and heal the most broken and hurting pieces within me. Help me experience your steadfast, healing love.

AT THE TABLE

Respect everyone, and love the family of believers.
Fear God, and respect the king.

1 PETER 2:17 NLT

At holiday dinners, entire families gather around dinner tables. Each member carries his or her own set of ideas and opinions. Personalities differ, and life experiences vary. In our humanness, we might carry hurts and disappointments about one another. Sometimes, these dinners are filled with love and acceptance, but other times they cause pain and further conflict. As we grow up, we realize that families are imperfect and often complicated.

The body of Christ is also an imperfect family. Each believer is different, with varying theological beliefs. Our differences have the ability to separate us, but God wants us to listen to one another, giving respect even if we passionately disagree. We are called to operate with hearts full of grace, despite our differences and weaknesses.

If we choose love, it can help us set aside our strife. Love brings unity and closeness, bridging gaps, so that we can live in harmony and peace, worshipping and serving together. A family is stronger with love at its center.

Jesus, as I grow, help me to live at peace with the church, despite disagreements. Help me to set aside my hurts and differences and choose to love. Let my focus be patience, kindness, and respect for the family of God. I am grateful that you love me despite my weakness; help me show that same love to everyone.

CHOOSE LOVE

"You have heard that it was said, 'Love your neighbor and hate your enemy.' But I tell you, love your enemies and pray for those who persecute you."

MATTHEW 5:43-44 NIV

One of the biggest struggles as a Christian is loving our enemies. Extending grace and understanding to those who have caused hurt is extremely difficult when our desire for justice is strong. Sometimes, we believe that our hate is justified, but it never is in the eyes of God. Each of our enemies has a name, a heart, a family. Like us, they need Jesus' love and grace.

Hate closes hearts and builds walls. Loving an enemy doesn't mean excusing or ignoring hurt—it means recognizing the value God gives them is the same as our value.

Jesus won his enemies over with his love, through service and companionship. He gave value to everyone. He walked with, talked to, and served his enemies. He was hated, rejected, and despised. He chose love and asked God to show mercy even to those who crucified him. We are called to do the same, despite the difficulty. No matter how justified we may feel in our anger, we are not given permission to hate. Instead, we are asked to choose to love.

Jesus, you see all of my pain. Let your care and love for me be enough. When I encounter enemies, help me to love them like you love them. Give me the courage to let go of my need for justice and soften my heart. Help me choose your love.

HOME SWEET HOME

*A man leaves his father and mother and is joined to his
wife, and the two are united into one.*

GENESIS 2:24 NLT

There is something sweet and bright about childhood
homes. When we are little, packing our bags and leaving
home is a distant and foreign concept. We can't imagine
leaving the comfort and protection of our parents.

God never intended us to stay at home forever. Before
we know it, our bags are packed, and we need that last bit of
courage and encouragement to walk out the door. Perhaps
we are heading to college, buying our first home, or getting
married, and the task is both exciting and daunting. Then,
homesickness hits. It doesn't matter how old we are or how
prepared we feel; the longing for home can take us by surprise.

It's scary to leave the familiar, but no matter what we do
or where we go, God is with us. He is safety, comfort, and
protection. When he lives in us, we know that we will be okay.
We don't have to live one day without him. He will walk us
through every new phase. For every plan he has, we know that
he will prepare and equip us to be successful. We can pack
our bags, knowing that we aren't beginning it alone.

**God, thank you that, even when I am called away from
my home and all of my comforts, you are my safety and
refuge. Remind me of that promise as I take the next step.**

TWO PATHS

"Enter through the narrow gate. For wide is the gate and broad is the road that leads to destruction, and many enter through it. But small is the gate and narrow the road that leads to life, and only a few find it."

MATTHEW 7:13-14 NIV

If given two paths, one difficult and the other easy, most of us would choose the easier path. Following God, however, is not easy, and there is only one path to him.

This path has obstacles and hardship. It asks us to give up our selfish ways and give our all to God. This path might bring us to our breaking point then rebuild us from the inside out. A path that is guaranteed to bring us closer to God in so many ways is a hard path to find, and many do not find it. It's our human nature to take the easy way out. The easy road doesn't lead to God, but ultimately to darkness and death.

In life, we constantly make little decisions that influence the path we walk. We can have courage, knowing that the Holy Spirit will sustain us on every step of our journey. There is so much joy in knowing that we don't walk alone. God is with us! There is beauty in the harder path, but we can't know that unless we walk it. Which will you walk: the path to life or the path to death?

Jesus, I want to follow you. I know that following you is not easy. Give me courage in this time. Thank you for sustaining me when I feel like giving up. You are my reward and my reason for this journey. Please, send your Holy Spirit to lead me and guide me.

CLEAN RECORD

As high as the heavens are above the earth,
so great is his love for those who fear him;
as far as the east is from the west,
so far has he removed our transgressions from us.
PSALM 103:11-12 NIV

If you break the law and are found guilty, your offenses go on a permanent criminal record. Background checks and Google searches will show a full account of all of your crimes and actions to anyone who looks for them. It doesn't matter where you go; that record will follow you for the rest of your life.

It will determine where you can work and what you can do. People will define you by it. They will judge your heart and your actions. The record doesn't show if you have made amends and changed your lifestyle. It only shows your wrongs.

Thankfully, God's love for us permanently destroys our criminal records, declaring us innocent. He remembers no wrongs, giving us a clear pass to start over and try again. We aren't defined by what we have done in the past; grace washes all that away. We aren't required to live in the past. We have permission to live in the present, restored, loved, and fully redeemed.

Thank you, God, for cleansing my wrongs in your love. Thank you for your grace, which gives me a future free from past judgments and sins. Thank you for restoring and redeeming our relationship. Remind me of my clean record every morning so that I may glorify you.

RIGHT OR LEFT?

You make known to me the path of life;
in your presence there is fullness of joy.

PSALM 16:11 ESV

There are many crossroads in life. We agonize about the future, obsessing over each step and wondering if we are walking in God's will for our life.

God's plan for our life has never been a mysterious secret. His purpose for every believer is to live in relationship with him. That relationship brings identity and joy. We can be content, knowing that our intimacy with God will naturally lead us at every turn.

Sometimes, it doesn't matter if we turn left or right. As long as God is the center of our lives, we are exactly where we should be. Trouble comes when we try to discover our purpose without God. Alone, we would search for it but not find it, unable to fill our emptiness. God is the only one who can fill us with a sense of purpose and direction.

Thank you, Lord, that regardless of what I do, you fill my days with sweet purpose. There is so much joy in walking this life with you. Keep me under your guiding arm, and open my eyes to your will.

LISTEN

The gatekeeper opens the gate for him, and the sheep hear his voice. He calls his own sheep by name and leads them out. When he has brought out all his own, he goes ahead of them, and the sheep follow him because they know his voice.

JOHN 10:3-4 NRSV

When planning for the future, you will receive tons of advice and opinions, wanted and unwanted. Well-intentioned friends and family and maybe even the cashier at the grocery store—how do you sift through everyone's voices and your own emotions?

Trying to weigh every option is overwhelming. Which is the right career, city, or college? Which one is God's will? What if you make the wrong step? Will you miss out? Silence those voices; they only bring confusion. Seek God first. Listen for him. Know his voice, and trust it.

The plans he has for you are good and better than you can imagine. Put your trust in God, and he will lead you. You will feel unshakeable peace as you move forward. He will open doors for you and oversee your progress. He will protect you, not abandon you. His is the only voice that matters, and he will help you figure out what is next.

Lord, thank you for going ahead of me—all I have to do is stop and listen for you. Thank you for your plans for me. Help me calm my heart, so that I can listen for your whisper. Let me trust in your voice above all others.

TRUE INTEGRITY

People with integrity walk safely,
but those who follow crooked paths will slip and fall.

PROVERBS 10:9 NLT

It's easy to have integrity when others are watching, but true integrity is being the same when we are alone, too. When we're alone, there is no one holding us to a higher standard, and we don't have to answer for our choices. We can choose honesty or deceit. In the moment, it might seem worth it to bend rules or lie for the right benefits.

Eventually, dishonesty and deceit are exposed, however. Sometimes, leaving our integrity at the door has long, life changing consequences. Our character is never worth exchanging for a desire, because those desires will damage our relationships. Trust is hard to rebuild, and respect takes a long time to earn.

When we choose to live honestly and cling to truth, we protect our character. If ever questioned, we are innocent. We can approach any situation with confidence, knowing that we are living by strong values and morals. People can look to us as are trustworthy and respectable, and we can walk as Christ's witnesses.

Jesus, I want to live for you when I am being watched and when I am not. Help me to be honest and truthful at all times. Help me live a life protected from blame and accusations, a life that honors you every moment of the day.

183

YOUR CALL MATTERS

"Rise and stand upon your feet, for I have appeared to you for this purpose, to appoint you as a servant and witness to the things in which you have seen me and to those in which I will appear to you."

ACTS 26:16 ESV

God called us to serve with him. We often think that means being a pastor or a missionary. Those are high, respectable callings, but not everyone is called to a life of ministry as an occupation. What about the rest of us?

Without warning, life gets busy: a job, school, a career, and a family soon fill our daily attention. Sometimes, we feel we don't have the time or energy to serve God or his people in big ways. We begin to wonder if we are truly important to God and his plans. In the monotony of life we begin to question if our lives hold value and significance to God. Yes, all of it matters.

When we choose to love another person in Jesus' name, we make a significant impact. Even if the actions seem small to us, they hold great purpose to God. We can be a loud testimony of God's power and love in our lives by living a quiet life for him. The smallest acts of kindness and service can have the greatest effect on others.

Jesus, help me to be content with the ways in which you ask me to serve you. I don't always see the ways you are using me for your purpose, but I trust that you are. I am so thankful that my life holds value and significance to you.

INVINCIBLE

Remember your Creator in the days of your youth.

ECCLESIASTES 12:1 NIV

God easily comes to mind when we are in trouble, our health is failing, or we are in desperate need. We call upon him to help, and he hears and delivers.

When we are young, the world is at our fingertips, and we feel invincible. We are often strong, healthy, and quick-minded. We are just beginning to discover our independence. We feel capable, untouchable, and independent. Options and opportunities lay at our feet. It is an exciting time, one that should be enjoyed. Youthfulness is a gift.

As we explore our freedom, we need to be careful not to walk away from our creator. No matter our abilities and strengths, we need him every day. He gave us those strengths and abilities. He alone will sustain our health, provide our daily needs, fill us with life and hope, and protect us from harm. Our independence doesn't mean independence from God. We shouldn't adopt the attitude that we don't need him. Instead, we should rely on him more, trusting him to guide and teach us as he orchestrates our lives.

God, please continue to lead me and teach me in this phase of my life. I need you when life is tough, but I also need you when it is easy. I am grateful for the path ahead, and I want to walk it with you. May I depend on you and not upon myself.

EXPOSURE

Humble yourselves before the Lord, and he will lift you up.
JAMES 4:10 NIV

Admitting sin and guilt is one of the hardest things to do. We have to humble our hearts, set aside our pride, and be open to others viewing our weakness. It is embarrassing and exposing, and, sometimes, fear of rejection and ridicule keeps us from seeking forgiveness and restitution.

In order to learn and grow, however, we must risk it. If we don't, our hearts can harden until they are resistant to the change that we need.

Vulnerability is a gift. When we humble ourselves before God, he receives us with love. When we miss the mark and go to him, we are met with grace and forgiveness. He wants to free us from sin and guilt. He wants to set us on our feet again and encourage us. The world may tear us down when we admit faults, but Jesus won't. He will take our soft heart and lovingly teach it. He will cover us with his love and build us up. We can run to him without fear.

God, keep my heart soft and teachable. I have so much to learn, and I want to change and grow. I am broken in my sin, but I am so thankful that your love covers and heals me. Please, surround me with your forgiveness and grace.

A COMFORTING PRESENCE

The Lord is my strength and shield.
I trust him with all my heart.
He helps me, and my heart is filled with joy.

PSALM 28:7 NLT

Think back to the last time you were struggling with something and a friend helped you walk through it. A friend's presence in a difficult time is a joy. Even if the only thing they physically did was listen to you and cry with you, they were there.

Presence is such a comfort, and God's presence is constant in every believer's life. Like a good friend, he helps us through dark and confusing times. His presence gives us strength and courage to push through. His friendship shields us from loneliness and pain. He makes heavy situations lighter and easier to handle.

We can trust that he will always be there when we need him. He is perfect faithfulness. Even when the world is crashing down around us, there is joy in knowing that we are never alone.

Lord God, thank you for being my friend and guiding me in every season of life. Your presence is a sweet relief during difficult and troubling times. Give me your strength and peace, and help me be aware of your presence when I feel alone.

LITTLE BLUE FISH

"Listen to me, you who know right from wrong, you who cherish my law in your hearts. Do not be afraid of people's scorn, nor fear their insults."

ISAIAH 51:7 NLT

Anytime we live differently than the rest of the world, we risk being laughed at, mocked, and insulted. Following Christ often requires us to go against the cultural grain, to stand apart from the crowd and to make decisions that aren't popular.

Every one of us wants to be accepted and loved, but oftentimes people who are different are rejected and shunned. It's not surprising that we can feel like a little blue fish in the sea, swimming against all the little red fishes. Being a Christian can be lonely and isolating.

Despite the consequences, we shouldn't conform for others' approval. If we truly love God, that love will propel us forward in obedience. Others' disapproval will not stick to the love that God drapes across our shoulders. It will fall away, and we will have peace, knowing that our identity is centered in God and not the world.

God, sometimes I'm weary of doing what is right when the world makes fun of my choices. Give me strength to continue walking in obedience. Remind me that others' opinions of me hold no value. You love me and are proud of me. I'm not alone in this world, because you are my constant companion and friend.

INTERNAL, EXTERNAL

Don't be concerned about the outward beauty of fancy hairstyles, expensive jewelry, or beautiful clothes. You should clothe yourselves instead with the beauty that comes from within, the unfading beauty of a gentle and quiet spirit, which is so precious to God.

1 PETER 3:3, 4 NLT

Being comfortable in our skin is a challenge. We don't always like what we see in the mirror. Men and women compare their images to the images of others, longing to look more athletic, better looking, or more desirable.

For some of us, rejecting the lie that we aren't enough is a daily struggle, and we search for perfection. If we aren't careful, our hearts will spiral into darkness. In our obsession, we put our hope into expensive brand name clothes, gadgets, and accessories, trying to match what we see on TV and online. Our hearts break when we realize that, no matter how hard we try to look beautiful on the outside, we don't feel beautiful on the inside.

The world does not define true beauty. God does. He decided long ago that we are incomparably beautiful. And the beauty of a loving spirit never ever fades. Instead of focusing on the external, we should look internally, letting God transform our hearts.

Jesus, please continue to show me what true beauty is. Thank you for loving me despite my faults. Help me to reject vanity and see the beauty that is already in me.

KING OF THE IMPOSSIBLE

God thunders wondrously with his voice;
he does great things that we cannot comprehend.

JOB 37:5 ESV

How often do we limit God's power in our life by forgetting who he is? He is the king of the world, yet we doubt that he can do mighty and wonderful things in our lives. We let our incomprehension box God into our human logic and ideas. There is no situation out of his control, yet we minimize his power and give into fear again and again. Fear steals our hope for change and rescue.

We can never understand the magnitude of his power, but we can trust him. He is the same God that parted the sea, calmed the storm, healed the blind, turned water to wine, fed thousands, and raised the dead. We don't have to understand his miracles to believe in the one who performed them. We can believe he can perform those miracles in our lives.

Even in the most impossible situations, we can wait in hope, trusting him. Taking hold of this hope, we can live by it as we look to tomorrow.

God, so often I forget who you are, especially when my life is in the midst of turmoil. You are the God of miracles, and you can—and will—perform miracles in my life. Help me live in expectant hope.

IN THIS SKIN

Charm is deceptive, and beauty does not last;
but a woman who fears the Lord will be greatly praised.

PROVERBS 31:30 NLT

We all desire to be known in some capacity. The question is: what do we want to be known for? Our charm? Our good looks? These gifts are highly valued in the world. Charisma and attractiveness can give us popularity and favor.

But what happens when beauty fades? What happens when our charm withers under hardship and time? What remains? Will ugliness lie underneath, or a heart of God? No amount of outward beauty can compare to the beauty that is made within by following Jesus.

Let love, grace, gentleness, kindness, and mercy be the beauty that defines us. We should aspire to be known by the way we treat others, for our accepting warmth and by our acts of service. This is beauty that doesn't die, and it has lasting impact. It is a beauty that all believers are able to have and share.

Jesus, I want to be known by the beauty that only comes from you. Grow faith, kindness, grace, and mercy in my heart. Help me not to obsess about my outward appearance and instead give attention into the heart underneath this skin. Only your love can take what is hard, selfish, and ugly and make it beautiful.

JOY STANDARDS

If they plant to satisfy their sinful selves, their sinful selves will bring them ruin. But if they plant to please the Spirit, they will receive eternal life from the Spirit.

GALATIANS 6:8 NCV

As we plan our futures, it's easy to get distracted by the world and its standards for success. If we aren't making a six-figure income and living in a large home, then we aren't successful. We are made to believe that these things will give us life and purpose so we work harder, sacrificing relationships for money and false security. Our energies focus on material comforts. Somehow, we believe that these things will bring us happiness.

Yet that joy never comes. And that's because God's standard for our lives is vastly different. He wants the focus to be on him alone and not on ourselves. When he says we can't serve two masters, he is right. What master will we choose to serve? The one who breathes life, or the one who is never satisfied?

It is always good to question our motives as we look ahead. Are we choosing to serve God or ourselves? Serving God will breathe life and joy into our lives. Serving ourselves will leave us continually dissatisfied, empty, and longing for more.

Lord, may my life's work be devoted to you and your purposes. In you, I will find deep joy and contentment. Help me not to be distracted by the material standards of success that this world sets.

JULY

This is the confidence that we have
toward him, that if we ask anything
according to his will he hears us.
And if we know that he hears us
in whatever we ask, we know that
we have the requests
that we have asked of him.

1 JOHN 5:14-15 ESV

UH OH, HIDE!

*Repent and return, so that your sins may be wiped away,
in order that times of refreshing may come from the
presence of the Lord.*

ACTS 3:19 NASB

Have you ever seen toddlers disobey and then try desperately to hide from their parents? It's cute because they are terrible at hiding, but it's heartbreaking, too, because there is no reason to hide from someone who loves you.

When we do something wrong, our natural instinct is to hide. We don't want to put our sin on display. We may feel embarrassment or deep shame mixed with a ton of regret. We want to disappear. We fear God's reaction and dread his disapproval. Rather than running to him, where we will find love and grace, we hide from him like little children.

Only in God's presence will we find relief from shame. When we find the courage to ask for forgiveness, he will wash us clean, restore us, and make us new. We have nothing to fear. God is not an angry or heavy-handed father. When we are hurting, God longs to wrap his comforting arms around us. He wants to meet us in our shame and embarrassment and free us from it, because we are his children and he loves us more than we can comprehend.

Jesus, when I mess up, I want to hide my shameful sins from you. I desperately need you to hold me, wipe away my tears, and tell me I am forgiven. Thank you for your unending grace and love that carries me through the worst of days.

THE FUTURE IS A MYSTERY

"I am the Lord, the God of all mankind.
Is anything too hard for me?"

JEREMIAH 32:27 NIV

God has your future well in view. The best way to handle this transition time is by developing your relationship with God and preparing for the coming unknown. How?

- Feed, rest, and exercise your body, to keep healthy and be able to think clearly
- Practice being in God's presence, praying and worshiping as you move through the day
- Forget yourself for a time, put down electronic devices, and reach out to serve others
- Read the Bible and sit in solitude daily, allowing God to interject words of direction and encouragement
- Share your thoughts and prayer needs with trusted friends
- Follow reliable advice regarding employment and financial stewardship
- Believe in God's faithfulness and be thankful for your blessings

In God's expert timing, he will lead you to the next part of your life's journey. Be ready.

Dear Lord, grant me patience and discipline to wait and prepare well, making the most of my transition time. Speak to me and help me hear your voice. Thank you for your abundant care.

FREEDOM OF GRACE

Sin is no longer your master, for you no longer live under the requirements of the law. Instead, you live under the freedom of God's grace.

ROMANS 6:14 NLT

Think back to the last time you sinned. Did you take hold of God's grace? Did you pick yourself back up? That is exactly what God wants us to do. Yet, so often when we make a mistake, we become discouraged and frustrated with ourselves. We begin to question if we will ever get it and wonder what is wrong with us.

In God's eyes, however, we are redeemed. Forgiven. Made new.

In our walk with God we will make mistakes. But when we mess up, we can grasp God's forgiveness and move on. We can recognize that we are saved by God's unending grace. We don't have to wallow in old sin patterns. We have freedom. His grace gives us hope—hope for victory over sin. We can trust that his work in our hearts is continual.

Jesus, you see me struggle, and you know every single one of my weaknesses. Thank you that you see beyond all that, into my heart. I am thankful for your grace. Help me to hold onto it and reject all the lies I feel when I make a mistake. Your grace is so undeserved and yet so life giving. Thank you for the courage to keep going when I feel defeated in my sin.

GIVER OF DREAMS

For still the vision awaits its appointed time;
it hastens to the end—it will not lie.
If it seems slow, wait for it;
it will surely come; it will not delay.

HABAKKUK 2:3 ESV

God is the giver of dreams. It is so amazing that his dreams and visions for us are more than we could possibly imagine or create on our own. God doesn't dangle dreams before us though to tease or taunt us. Rather, he shares his dreams with us so that we can partake in his vision and so that we can see and know His heart for us and for his people.

Our timing in not God's timing, though. We will never always understand why sometimes we have to wait years to see them come true. But we can trust him in the wait. His word is honest and unchanging.

We can trust that our longing has a purpose. We can trust that while we wait for God and for his dreams our reliance on him will grow. And we can trust that our faith in him will be strengthened and that he will not disappoint us.

Jesus, sometimes I am so impatient for the dreams that I sit upon and wait for. Give me patience and increase my trust in you and in your vision for my life. Help me be steadfast in the wait. Thank you for the dreams you have given me; they bring me hope and joy.

A LITTLE LIGHT

Your word is a lamp for my feet,
a light on my path.

PSALM 119:105 NIV

Navigating our way in darkness is nearly impossible without bumping into things, stumbling, and falling. That's why we keep dark places lit with lamps and night-lights. We depend on light in order to know where we are going. Without it, we can't be certain that we'll get to our destination without harm.

In the pitch dark, even a little bit of light brings direction and saves us from potential bruising. It's silly to try to get to our destination without aid. Yet, how often though do we try to live life blindly because we are confident in our own abilities to see and find our own way in darkness?

When our future gets confusing and dark, only God's light will bring us through the darkness unharmed and untouched. We don't have to find our way in the dark, however, because God is our light. We can put our confidence in him because he loves us. His word is our light. His voice illuminates our paths.

Thank you, God, for your Word. Thank you that your voice safeguards me from becoming hurt and lost in the darkness. I am so thankful that you love me so much and that you are my lamp on every journey.

SELF-RELIANCE

My soul, wait silently for God alone,
For my expectation is from Him.
He only is my rock and my salvation;
He is my defense;
I shall not be moved.

PSALM 62:5-6 NKJV

From a very early age, we are taught how self-reliance and independence is something to be admired. Strength is idolized, while weakness is seen to be something to be ashamed of and embarrassed about. As adults we learn that it is frowned upon to ask for help or admit that we are struggling.

So we put our dependence on ourselves. But we were never created to live in our own strength. In fact, if we try, we are bound to fail and stumble. We were created with a deep need for God's presence in our life. Jesus wants to be our strength, our hope, and our refuge.

We will always find strength when we depend on him. He will sustain us in our weakness and bring us through every trial and trouble. In our struggles we can look to him to help us, and he will.

Jesus, I am tired of trying to be strong. And I am weary of trying to prove to others that I am capable, when, in truth, I desperately need your helping hand in my life. So I wait. I wait for your help. I am thankful for your faithfulness to me. Tear my independent spirit from me, and let my faith rest in you.

BOMBARDED WITH LIES

Sanctify them in the truth;
Your word is truth.

JOHN 17:17 NASB

Every day we are bombarded with lies that are intended to destroy and harm us, and keep us away from the goodness of God. Whispers of deceit tell us that we aren't good enough, strong enough, or worthy of God's love and grace.

The only way to combat these lies is with the truth. And God's word is truth. It will wash us clean from all these lies. The truth will reveal that God's grace has set us apart from the world and that we were made into new creations.

So when lies make us feel that we are less than worthy, we can run to God's Word to renew and refresh us. His truth will seep into our pores and make us strong again. His truth will lift us up out of despair and discouragement and grow confidence in our hearts.

God, I am so thankful for your Word, given to me and filled with healing truth. I will not let lies stop me from pursuing you and your plans for me life. Thank you for the work you are doing in my life, and I reject any lie that tells me otherwise. I cling to your word, your truth, and your love.

AVOID A FIGHT

Avoiding a fight is a mark of honor;
only fools insist on quarreling.

PROVERBS 20:3 NLT

"Did not!"
"Did too!"
"Did not!"
"Did too!"

And round and round the arguing goes. Have you ever known someone who is always looking to pick a fight? When you enter into an argument with someone like that, it only brings you down to their level. A heated exchange is almost never productive. Instead it resolves nothing and ends up hurting everyone involved.

The best thing to do is to hold your tongue and say nothing. It takes two to fight, right? So when you don't reply to their answer with one of your own, the arguing starts to die down. Make it your goal to keep out of any foolish arguments. Staying quiet during an argument rarely makes you look stupid. Instead it will earn you respect.

God, help me not to get caught up in fights and foolish arguments. I know that in the end they will only bring harm. Help me to love people instead of fighting with them. Help me to represent you well.

LOVE THE UNLOVELY

"If you love those who love you, what reward do you have? Do not even the tax collectors do the same?"

MATTHEW 5:46 ESV

It's pretty easy to love the people that are popular. We're naturally drawn to people who are attractive, rich, and well-liked. On the other hand, it's difficult to go out of our comfort zones and love someone who is unpopular, uncool, and not well-off. Some people can be downright annoying or embarrassing to be seen with. Who are you trying to impress with your friendships? God? Or the people around you?

Take a moment to write down the names of five people that either upset you or are unlovely. Now make it your mission to pray for those five people every day. Then, each day, choose one name from the list and ask God to show you how to love that person in a specific, practical way. When you make a commitment to love, it won't go unnoticed. How awesome would it be to catch the eye of God!

Lord, I want to befriend those who need friends. I want to be kind to those who most people aren't kind to. Bring to my mind the people that I need to reach out to. Show me how to love like you.

GUIDED BY HONESTY

A good man is guided by his honesty;
the evil man is destroyed by his dishonesty.

PROVERBS 11:3 TLB

Have you ever been caught in a lie? People tell lies for many reasons—to save face, to make someone feel better, or to escape punishment. But the reality is that no lie goes without a consequence. One of the biggest consequences is that anyone found in a lie becomes very difficult to trust again.

Truth is always worth whatever you sacrifice to tell it. You might feel pain for a moment by exposing whatever you'd hoped to cover up, but your obedience to God won't go unrewarded. In some ways, your honesty will guide you to success because people will learn to trust you.

God, I want to be someone who is guided by honesty and not a fool who is destroyed by dishonesty. I don't want to tell lies and end up hurting those around me by my selfishness. Help me always to choose the truth.

BECOMING PERFECT

Let patience have its perfect work, that you may be perfect and complete, lacking nothing.

JAMES 1:4 NKJV

Growing up is a process—and not always an easy one. Maturity comes with a price; it's fashioned through difficulty and learned through error. Wisdom can't be arrived at gently; it must be earned by patience, perseverance, and steady trust.

When trouble comes in your life, remember that it's just another necessary hurdle in your process of maturity. You might feel weak when you're walking through a difficult time, but standing on the other side of it you will feel stronger and more firmly planted than ever before. That's a promise! Remember, you don't have to face hard things alone— surrender your life to God and he will lead you through.

Thank you, God, for leading me through all kinds of difficulty and helping me toward maturity. I know that no matter how hard all of this is, it will be worth it. Thank you for never leaving my side. Help me to lean on you more.

CALL TO HIM

I was in trouble, so I called to the Lord.
The Lord answered me and set me free.

PSALM 118:5 NCV

Many times when we are in trouble, our first instinct is to hide from God. Maybe our trouble is a result of sin or our own stupidity and we don't want to face God. We end up being ashamed and afraid of him, avoiding him when we truly need him the most.

But God is our Father. He's not going to shut us out in our trouble—he wants to lift us out of it. His love for us is greater than any sin. His grace can handle whatever we might have done. When we are in trouble, instead of hiding from God, we should be calling out to him. When our life is falling apart, he will rebuild it and put it back together. When our hearts are broken, he will overwhelm us with his unconditional love. Where sin has trapped us, he will rescue us and set us free.

God, when I'm in trouble I feel afraid to come to you. I don't want you to be disappointed in me. I hate that I still sin, and I don't like causing you pain. When those times come, that's when I need you most, Lord. Set me free.

A BIG STEP

Listen, my son, to your father's instruction
and do not forsake your mother's teaching.
They are a garland to grace your head
and a chain to adorn your neck.

PROVERBS 1:8-9 NIV

Leaving home for the first time can feel wonderful and exhilarating, but it can also be overwhelming. Overnight, you are independent. Suddenly, you are responsible for all of your needs. You have to make all the big decisions independently. You are navigating the world without your parents' help. Nervously, you begin to question if you are ready for such a big step.

Do you have what it takes?

Be encouraged in those moments. It may feel like you are alone, but you are not. Your parents and mentors have been preparing you for this phase in your life from the day you were born. Their wisdom and counsel will follow you as you make decisions for the first time. Their teaching in your life is a gift. Use it, and keep it close. And, above all, you will never be alone because God will go with you.

Lord, thank you for giving me people in my life who are wise and intelligent. I am grateful for their teachings because navigating life independently is made a little easier because of them. I feel equipped and prepared to go wherever you may call me.

A LOOSE CANNON

Those who are careful about what they say
keep themselves out of trouble.

PROVERBS 21:23 NCV

You may or may not be a history buff or be particularly interested in ancient nautical warfare, but, in either case, you may find this interesting.

From the seventeenth to the nineteenth centuries, ships were armed with enormous cannons that when fired had a tremendous recoil. To avoid damage, the cannons were mounted on rollers and tied securely with ropes. A "loose cannon" was one that had jerked itself away from its restraints and rolled dangerously around the deck, damaging everything in its wake.

Have you ever felt like your tongue is a loose cannon? If so, join the club! Realize that the only solution is the power of Jesus and a commitment to think before you speak!

Lord, help me to control my tongue and be careful about what I say.

KINDERGARTEN

Be kind to each other, tenderhearted, forgiving one
another, just as God through Christ has forgiven you.
EPHESIANS 4:32 NLT

Likely some fifteen years before you even started school, an American minister and author wrote a series of essays about the important things a child learns in Kindergarten: be fair; share; be nice; don't hit people; and say you're sorry. Hopefully, you learned these things when it was your turn.

Similarly, the Bible is just as simple and straightforward. You don't have to wonder what God is saying. You just have to read it and obey: be kind; be compassionate and understanding; and forgive others just as Christ forgave you.

Think of the people in your life you admire the most and see if you recognize any of these qualities. As you say good-bye to your childhood and launch into adulthood, recall what you saw in those people and emulate it.

Lord, thank you for your Word that gives such clear direction. I want my life to be a life of kindness, compassion, and forgiveness. I want to follow in your steps.

FORGIVENESS IS . . .

Bearing with one another, and forgiving one another,
if anyone has a complaint against another; even as Christ
forgave you, so you also must do.

COLOSSIANS 3:13 NKJV

Forgiveness is hard. Even without apologies, it is important to forgive. Grudges can consume you, and unforgiveness can hold power over your life. But forgiveness takes your life back.

Let's review what forgiveness is and isn't. Forgiveness is turning the situation over to the Lord and letting him deal with it. Forgiveness is not playing the victim. Forgiveness is for our healing. Forgiveness is not denying that wrong was done.

Jesus calls us to forgive as he has forgiven us, over and over and over. We know that we have forgiven someone when their name no longer makes us anxious or angry. Jesus died so that we would be reconciled with him and with one another. So don't give up or walk away too soon.

Lord, I don't want to carry this hurt anymore. Help me let this go so that I can have my life back and experience your perfect peace. I trust you, and I want to give others the grace you have given me.

ADOPTED

Father of orphans and protector of widows is God in his holy habitation.

PSALM 68:5 NRSV

This verse has brought comfort to millions of people. Perhaps you've lost a parent yourself, or know someone who has and you understand his or her unique needs. God is aware of it all. Think of it! Almighty God, who spoke the universe into existence, is personal and compassionate enough to be mindful of those in need.

And God wants everyone to know. In the days ahead, remember that you have a heavenly father who dwells in his holy habitation.

He will protect you, support you, and be your champion! Be mindful of those around you who may be alone or hurting. God may want to use you as his instrument of comfort and protection.

Thank you, God, for being my Father and for making me your child. Help me to trust you completely in the days ahead.

IT'S JUST NOT FAIR!

"For I, the Lord, love justice;
I hate robbery and wrongdoing.
In my faithfulness I will reward my people
and make an everlasting covenant with them."

ISAIAH 61:8 NIV

Do you remember when, as a child, things didn't go your way? You'd lament, "It's just not fair!" And that's not only a childish thought because so much in life really isn't fair—all things are definitely not equal.

Throughout your life you will encounter situations that seem completely unfair to you, and perhaps they are. Instead of trying to figure it out yourself, bring your concern to God. He is always just, impartial, objective, and fair-minded—he simply can be no other way.

Commit to following God no matter what. Love justice like he does; be honest and forthright in all your relationships; and hate wrongdoing and be as faithful to him as he is to you!

Thank you, Lord, for establishing a covenant of faithfulness with me. I can count on you. Help me to be honest and fair in my dealings with others.

211

PARTNER CHOICE

An excellent wife, who can find?
For her worth is far above jewels.
PROVERBS 31:10 NASB

There are some girls who dream of marriage from the time they are little. They play house; they play with their dolls; and they daydream about a beautiful wedding and a life of happiness with their prince charming.

Marriage is probably in your future at some point, and your choice of a partner is the second most important decision you will ever make! The first, of course, is your decision to give your heart and life to Jesus Christ. In both cases, you will have made a lifelong commitment, and there should be no turning back!

Men, don't settle for a bride who is not committed to living for Christ with the same intensity you are. She will be a rare find, indeed. Ladies, develop your relationship with the Lord and find contentment in your singleness. Focus on being all you can be for the Lord, and when the time is right, he will bring you a most excellent husband!

Lord, I commit my life and my relationships to you. Be Lord over my affections and help me guard my heart from the wrong attachments. I want to be an excellent partner to my future spouse!

FIRST LOVE

Yet I hold this against you:
You have forsaken the love you had at first.

REVELATION 2:4 NIV

There is nothing sadder than seeing a relationship that has grown cold. Songs have been sung, books written, and movies produced about heartbreaking stories of love that has died.

The letter to the church of Ephesus in Revelation 2 speaks of a similar problem. They had grown cold in their love for God and others. They were busy doing God's work; they had patiently endured hardship; and they hated wickedness and exposed evil when they saw it. Yet God had this one complaint against them: they had abandoned the love they once had.

Maintaining a loving relationship takes intentionality; it doesn't just happen. Love for family and friends grows when you spend time with them. You have to talk with them and do things together. Love for God is the same. As you get increasingly busy in the coming days, don't neglect your relationship with the Lord. Don't grow cold and indifferent. Listen, because God is calling you back!

Lord, help me in the days ahead to keep my relationship with you first. I don't want to grow cold by neglecting my relationship with you.

ALTOGETHER DIFFERENT

Have mercy on me, O God,
because of your unfailing love.
Because of your great compassion,
blot out the stain of my sins.

PSALM 51:1 NLT

If you've grown up following God and obeying his commands, it might be hard for you to watch others turn their back on him. People that you once knew loved God seem to have walked away. You might be wondering, How does God view people like that? What does he think of them?

King David, someone who was described as a person after God's own heart, turned his back on God for a time. He stole and had someone murdered. What did God think of him? Well, God loved him enough to send someone to confront David. God is altogether different than we are. Where our patience has run out, his loving kindness and persevering love are still running at full throttle. Instead of criticizing others, we have the privilege of continuing to show God's unfailing love to those who've turned away from him. Maybe the love we show them will bring them back to God.

Father, thank you for your heart of compassion and for welcoming even the most rebellious person back to you. Help me to show that same compassion to others.

A SOURCE YOU CAN TRUST

Faith comes from hearing,
and hearing through the word of Christ.

ROMANS 10:17 ESV

Rumors are just rumors until you hear it for yourself from a source you trust. Anyone who ever played "telephone" as a young girl knows how words can get twisted and changed as they go from one person to the next. If you want to know if your friend really said or did what she's being accused of, ask her.

The same goes for God. We can't call him up and ask him, but we can read his sacred text and find out what he said. Everything he ever said, did, or wants us to know is written down and available for our study. Our faith in God grows by hearing what he did, who he is, and what he says. Our source is the Bible. Need more faith? Read the Word. Need more truth, guidance, and wisdom? They're all there.

God, thank you for making sure that everything I need to know is written in your Word. Guide me toward the lessons and truths you most want me to learn. Help my faith to grow.

CHOOSING WELL

"Today I have given you the choice between life and death, between blessings and curses. Now I call on heaven and earth to witness the choice you make. Oh, that you would choose life, so that you and your descendants might live!"

DEUTERONOMY 30:19 NLT

God is intimately interested in your choices. He may not be on the edge of his seat wondering if you'll have a PB&J or a turkey sandwich for lunch, but make no mistake, that decision to cheat or not, lie or be truthful, date or wait, he can't wait to see what you decide.

You know God has plans for you, but do you also know that the final choice rests with you? He guides and directs but you decide, and all of heaven and earth are waiting to see how it turns out.

Lord, sometimes I wish I didn't have to choose. I wish you'd just make the hard decisions for me, but I know that's not how it works. Thank you for my freedom to choose and for guiding me to choose well.

EARN A GOOD DAY?

Lord, every morning you hear my voice;
Every morning, I tell you what I need,
and I wait for your answer.

PSALM 5:3 NCV

If you've grown up in a church setting, you've likely been told to spend some time with God every day. Some people refer to this as a "quiet time" and others call it "devotions." Perhaps that is why you are reading this book right now—because you are having devotions for the day.

Spending time talking and listening to God every day is a great lifelong habit to create. However, just because you have taken the time to meet with God doesn't mean you earn a great day from him. In fact, devotions aren't meant to earn you anything. Spending time with God is meant to get you in the habit of talking and listening to your Father. The more you talk to him and study his Word, the easier it will be to hear him during the day, on rough days, happy days, and days when you need some help.

Thank you, Lord, that you hear my voice in the morning and all throughout the day. Help me set aside time each day to talk with you.

217

THIRSTY

My soul thirsts for God, for the living God;
When shall I come and appear before God?

PSALM 42:2 NASB

God designed your body to need food and drink. Eating and drinking gives you the physical energy you need to function throughout the day. To stop eating and drinking means getting thirsty, hungry, and eventually dying.

The same is true for your soul: it needs to be fed and watered as well. This kind of eating and drinking means spending time with the Father. It means letting him love you. It means turning to him and learning his Word. It means sitting in his presence and listening to his voice. When you neglect this regularly, you allow restlessness, insecurities, and fears to take hold in your heart. Make a habit of "feeding" your soul so you'll grow spiritually strong.

Father, remind me to come and feast at your table daily: not to prove my spirituality to you, others, or myself, but simply because you invite me to spend time with you.

IT'S NOT OVER YET

He who testifies to these things says,
"Yes, I am coming soon."
Amen. Come, Lord Jesus.
REVELATION 22:20 NIV

Turn on the TV or your smart phone these days and all that seems to come up is a string of discouraging news. Between news about wars, famines, modern day slavery, and natural catastrophes, it's hard not to have a heavy heart. It might seem like the times we are living in are getting darker and darker. And in many ways, they are.

But the best news is this: things aren't over yet! Jesus prophesied in Matthew 24 that many difficult things would happen before his return. You can have hope that Jesus is coming back. He'll have the final say and will make all things new. Ask God to open your eyes to the ways he's working around you. While evil sometimes *seems* to be winning, grace is at work everywhere.

Dear Lord, thank you that you have the final say in the world around me. Help me to keep my eyes open for the good things you're doing every day and to keep hoping for the day when you'll return.

UNDERSTOOD

You have searched me, Lord,
and you know me.

PSALM 139:1 NIV

Have you ever been misunderstood? If so, it is not a positive feeling. Perhaps someone misjudged your motives or questioned a decision you made and you were left speechless or perhaps confused yourself. There's something inside of us that longs to be known—to have someone in our lives who "gets us."

Psalm 139 is a powerful expression of God's intimate involvement in our lives. We are an open book to him.

He knows where we are, what we are thinking, and always has us in his view. He knows our thoughts and what we are going to say. He surrounds us from every direction no matter where we are!

I am overwhelmed, Lord, by the knowledge that you are always with me. As my creator, you naturally understand me through and through. Help me to live in such a way that I am unashamed to be known by you. And as you search my heart, I pray that you would find it pure.

AGAPE

Dear friends, let us love one another, for love comes from God. Everyone who loves has been born of God and knows God.

I JOHN 4:7 NIV

Love is probably the most overused word in the English language. It has so many meanings, from loving peanut butter on toast to loving a pet cat to loving Christmas. The kind of love John refers to in this verse is of a different sort, however: Agape love.

Agape love is a love that originates in God, because God is love. This love keeps on loving even when the loved one is unresponsive, unkind, unlovable, and unworthy. It is unconditional love. This is the love God has for us. When we are born again and the Spirit of God takes up residence in us, we then can love in the same way. We cannot produce this kind of love ourselves—it is a gift of God.

You will encounter many new people in the days ahead and some of them will be difficult to like, much less love. As a child of God, you must draw on his love that resides in you. Agape love is not necessarily a feeling of affection. It is more of an intention—a commitment to think about the other's well-being and happiness more than your own. Can you show others that you are a Christian by your love?

Lord, help me love others as you love me. Help me to show kindness and patience toward those who do not reciprocate it. You have given me the gift of your love. Give me grace to be the channel of that love to others.

THE BOTTOM LINE

Let us hear the conclusion of the whole matter:
Fear God and keep His commandments,
For this is man's all.

ECCLESIASTES 12:13 NKJV

Sometimes all we need to hear is the bottom line. We need to skip all the details and minutia and get right down to the main thing. That's what Solomon did at the end of his book. He took twelve chapters to philosophize on the futility of life without God and then got to the fundamentals.

Remember, this king had it all—fame, riches, and wisdom. Yet he opened and closed his book with "everything is meaningless, completely meaningless." Perhaps he wrote this later in life and was reflecting on his mistakes and failures, wishing he had lived a simpler, more God-focused life.

Life does get complicated. But when you get right down to it, there's only one thing you really need to know and that's to fear God and keep his commandments. Nothing else is as important. Never let that truth leave you—hold it fast because this is your whole duty. Fear God. Do what he tells you.

Lord, I love how your word is so straightforward and uncomplicated. Help me carry out your mandate to me because I know as I obey I will be blessed.

DIRECTIONS

He guides me in the paths of righteousness
For His name's sake.

PSALM 23:3 NASB

Have you ever gotten lost? Many people are directionally challenged, and following a map or even simple verbal directions leaves them very confused. In contrast, some people have an internal map that makes getting places so much easier!

Here, the psalmist is not speaking about this type of dilemma. This is about a spiritual truth. The road we need to travel on is one of righteousness. The guidance we need doesn't come from a map—it comes from God.

God's desire for your life is that you walk with him, that you maintain a right standing with Him at all times, and that every choice you make brings honor to his name. This sounds like a tall order! But just remember you are not alone in this—you have a guide who will direct each of your steps as you allow him to.

Thank you, Lord, for being my guide and for leading me in the paths of righteousness. Help me to heed your direction and never to wander off on my own!

BRAGGING

Let someone else praise you, not your own mouth—
a stranger, not your own lips.

PROVERBS 27:2 NLT

It's so cute when children brag: "Look at me! Look at me! Look at me!" We can't help but share the exuberance and respond with our congratulations.

It's not so cute when adults do the same.

As you probably know, the book of Proverbs is packed full of good advice. Proverbs is really a Biblical collection of wisdom for all ages and stations in life with the purpose of teaching wisdom to God's people. They are not promises as such, but truisms that are short, clever, and easy to remember. This one certainly is: just don't brag. Don't toot your own horn. Let someone else do it!

Thank you, Lord, for the wisdom you offer me in the book of Proverbs. Help me to remain humble even in the middle of my greatest achievements. I want to give you glory in all I do and give you credit for what you have allowed me to accomplish.

AUGUST

May he give you the power to
accomplish all the good things
your faith prompts you to do.

2 THESSALONIANS 1:11 NLT

LIFE IS FLEETING

You do not know what will happen tomorrow! Your life is like a mist. You can see it for a short time, but then it goes away.

JAMES 4:14 NCV

The Bible makes it clear that life is fleeting. We may convince ourselves that we have lots of time and an unlimited future, but, in truth, our time here on the earth is short. Although we can make plans for the days and years to come, only God knows the span of time we will be given. That's why it's important to make the most of our "mist."

Grocery stores have automatic hydrating systems that put out a light spray every few minutes over the green leafy vegetables. When the lettuce and spinach start to look droopy, a quick shower perks them right back up. That little bit of well-timed moisture is all those veggies need to stay healthy and appealing.

Comparing our lives to mist may sound disheartening at first. But far from being insignificant, our brief lives can bring great refreshment to those around us every day. We can sprinkle hope into dry seasons and thirsty souls. Our consistent, gentle influence can have an effect that carries into eternity.

Lord, help us see how precious each day is. Give us wisdom to make the most of every opportunity to bring hope and healing to the people around us. Thank you for this life and a future eternity with you.

COMMON SENSE OR WISDOM?

Sensible people keep their eyes glued on wisdom,
but a fool's eyes wander to the ends of the earth.

PROVERBS 17:24 NLT

Common sense tells us to wear a coat when it's ten degrees below zero outside. It reminds us not to drive on an empty tank and to refrain from eating the whole package of Oreos. For life's bigger decisions, we need more than common sense. We need wisdom. Where can we find it?

The television bombards us with a type of worldly wisdom that changes as fast as the click of the remote can change channels. In a matter of minutes, the Internet can offer our eyes an opportunity to wander from one end of the earth to the other. And, of course, there are the voices of social media, which aren't always reliable sources of truth.

If we are seeking God-sense, then we need to fix our eyes on God's wisdom, Scripture. It takes focus and concentration to ignore the distractions vying for our attention. But by keeping our Bibles open and our eyes glued to its wisdom, we can avoid a lot of nonsense.

Lord, thank you for the guidance and instruction that is found in your Word. Help us keep our eyes on you and find the answers we are seeking by listening to your voice in the pages of Scripture.

EASY SWINGING

My guilt has overwhelmed me
like a burden too heavy to bear.

PSALM 38:4 NIV

If you've ever been to a baseball game, you've probably seen the batter take a few practice swings before stepping up to the plate. Often, the player will put a heavy ring on the bat before his warm-ups. That way, when he steps into the batter's box, the bat feels light in his hands and the swing is easy.

It would be ridiculous for the batter to insist on keeping that heavy weight on his bat as he faces the pitcher. Certainly, his quickness would be hindered and his ability to succeed would be greatly compromised.

When we carry a load of guilt over past mistakes and unwise choices, it slows us down. We can't function at our best. Yet many of us insist on dragging that weight around without realizing it has become a great hindrance. God is faithful, and he will not only forgive our sins but will also graciously lift the weight of guilt that we were not meant to bear.

Lord, today we choose to lay down the heaviness of guilt that we've been carrying. Thank you for being faithful to forgive our sins and to cleanse us from guilt. Help us to step into this day with the joy that comes from freedom in Christ.

NEVER DISAPPOINTED

Give thanks to the Lord, for he is good,
for his steadfast love endures forever.

PSALM 136:1 ESV

Things just don't seem to last. When your car begins to make that clunking sound and smoke begins to roll out from under the hood, you know cars don't last. When your phone falls out of your pocket and the screen is so badly cracked you can't send texts without shedding blood, you know gadgets don't last. Lifelong friendships, the keeping of promises, and commitment to a cause are hard to come by in this world.

Not so with God. His love never disappoints, and this verse gives three big reasons why. First, God's love is steadfast, which means it is unwavering and rock-solid dependable. Second, God's love is enduring—it sticks with us and never gives up on us. And third, God's love is a forever love, guaranteed for all time. God can love like that because his character is flawless and his capacity to love is limitless.

If you need something to thank the Lord for today, offer him your gratitude for his steadfast, enduring, and forever love.

Thank you, Lord, for your steady, faithful love. In a world where nothing seems to last, it's nice to know we can depend on you to continue loving us unconditionally and eternally.

ALL OF ME

*Therefore, I urge you, brothers and sisters, in view of God's
mercy, to offer your bodies as a living sacrifice, holy and
pleasing to God—this is your true and proper worship.*

ROMANS 12:1 NIV

When a bride and groom exchange vows, they offer
themselves completely to each other. The groom doesn't say,
"I give you my bank account," and the bride doesn't say, "I
give you my car." They present themselves to each other as a
whole package—body, soul, spirit, mind, bank account, and
car. In a good marriage, nothing is held back.

God, in his mercy, didn't withhold anything from us but
gave his one and only son to die in our place. In light of that
supreme sacrifice, we are encouraged to present a life-filled
offering of ourselves to God without holding back. This kind of
all-in commitment is true worship and delights his heart.

Why are we urged to offer our bodies? Simply because
our bodies carry around the rest of us—spirit, soul, mind, and
heart. If we offer our bodies, everything else comes along.

**Lord, I offer you my body and all that goes with it.
I present to you my soul and my spirit, my will and my
personality, and my hopes and my dreams for the future.
Help me to withhold nothing and trust you in everything.**

BASED ON KINDNESS

Then he saved us—not because we were good enough to
be saved but because of his kindness and pity—by washing
away our sins and giving us the new joy of the indwelling
Holy Spirit.

TITUS 3:5 TLB

Report cards have changed a lot over the years. An "A-B-C-D-F" grading scale used to be standard, but some schools have now gone to a "Satisfactory/Progressing/Unsatisfactory" system of grading. An "S" in Math, for example, means the student has done enough to pass and has satisfied the basic requirements.

If God graded us on how good we were, we'd all get a big fat red "F." Or perhaps a "U." We all come up short of his high standard of holiness. Besides that, "enough" is a hard target to hit. How do we know when we are good enough, or smart enough, or "satisfactory" enough?

It's a good thing God's plan of salvation is based on his kindness and not on our achievements. Otherwise, we might be tempted to boast and take credit for it ourselves. God took pity on us and created a system based on his work of forgiveness, which is more than enough.

Lord, thank you for finding a way to save us based on your goodness and not ours. Thank you for giving us the Holy Spirit, who keeps us progressing toward holiness.

BLESSED IN GRIEVING

"They are blessed who grieve, for God will comfort them."
MATTHEW 5:4 NCV

Most of us don't think of grief as a blessing. Loss can derail us for a time, whether it's the death of a loved one, the breakup of a relationship, or a move away from a familiar place to a new place. These major upheavals can be devastating. Feelings of loss can come in smaller ways, too. Missing out on an anticipated event or realizing a dream isn't going to come true can cause intense sadness. Where is the blessing in that?

When small children are sick, their parents suffer right along with them. Although they aren't happy about their child's illness, they don't mind the extra snuggles and the chance to comfort their little one. Those can be tender times, deepening the bond of their love.

In the same way, God doesn't take pleasure in our sorrow. But in times of grief, we are often more open to his love and comfort. Our brokenness brings him near—close enough to feel his presence and sense his strength.

Lord, your arms are a safe and secure place when we're experiencing pain. May we learn to draw near to you in those moments and receive your comfort.

TRUSTING HEART

The Lord is my strength and my shield;
My heart trusted in Him, and I am helped;
Therefore my heart greatly rejoices,
And with my song I will praise Him.

PSALM 28:7 NKJV

You know how it is when you are sick. You just want to get some medicine that will make you feel better. It doesn't matter to you that the doctor's scribble on the prescription is illegible. You don't think about the millions of pills the pharmacist has to pick from to get you the right ones.

You don't even hesitate to put that little tablet in your mouth and swallow it. You are confident that you are being helped. That's a lot of trust.

God is trustworthy and stands ready to help. When you're tired and overwhelmed, his strength will sustain you. When you are fearful or anxious, his shield will protect you. As you recognize his faithful support in your times of need, your trusting heart will become a rejoicing heart—and your rejoicing heart will break out in praise.

Lord, you are my strength and my shield. Teach my heart to trust in you more and more. Thank you for helping me in ways I don't even realize. I praise you, God, for your goodness to me.

DOUBT THE DOUBT

I cried out, "I am slipping!"
but your unfailing love, O Lord, supported me.
When doubts filled my mind,
your comfort gave me renewed hope and cheer.

ISAIAH 94:18-19 NLT

We need to learn to doubt our doubts instead of doubting our beliefs. The devil wants to get us on the slippery slope of skepticism. It's an old tactic, going back to the Garden of Eden, when the serpent caused Eve to question God's words. That crafty snake planted a seed of doubt in Eve's mind, which led to her major slip-up and downfall. Doubt is a temptation to disbelieve in the goodness of God. A voice hisses in our ear, *If God really cared, he would . . .*

When we begin to doubt and feel ourselves sinking down, the first thing we need to do is look at the cross. No one has ever done more to prove the extent of their love than Jesus did at Calvary. God's love and care for us never needs to be questioned. That was settled at the cross.

Let's not doubt our beliefs. Let's believe our beliefs and doubt our doubts.

Lord, thank you for your unfailing love, which reaches out to support us when we cry out for help. Keep our minds sharp and able to discern truth from error. Take away our doubts and fill us instead with your hope and joy.

WORLD WITH LIMITS

"Then I will heal you of your faithlessness;
my love will know no bounds,
for my anger will be gone forever."

HOSEA 14:4 NLT

We live in a world with limits. Most of us have learned how to stay within certain boundaries. We have to obey speed limits if we want to be safe and avoid seeing red flashing lights in our rear view mirror. Spending limits keep us from buying more than we can afford and getting into debt. Time limits give us deadlines to complete an assignment or finish a job. The government even puts restrictions on how many fish we can catch.

We need these boundaries because if they weren't in place, we would probably drive too fast, spend too much, and waste a lot of time. We might even get greedy out on the lake.

Limits are not necessary with God because he never abuses his power. He perfectly strong and perfectly good. When it comes to dealing with his children, his love is limitless, inexhaustible and boundless.

Lord, help us to never limit your work in our lives. Give us the capacity to receive your love in greater measure, although it is so great that we will never see the end of it. Let us become a reflection of you, as we love others with that same kind of extravagant love.

POWER TO SAVE

"Get rid of all moral filth and the evil that is so prevalent and humbly accept the word planted in you, which can save you."

LUKE 10:27 NIV

What we put into our minds has power over us. Every movie, video game, and what books we read have an effect. When we are taking in things that are evil—or not honoring to God—we destroy our minds and our heart. That sounds extreme because it really feels harmless. What happens subtly below the surface isn't harmless. We are slowly, but deeply, being affected by everything we take in.

When we focus on things that are filled with God's truth and that bring messages of purity, life, and light, then our minds are being built up. We are becoming better from what we are hearing and seeing. The fruit of that will come out in our lives. When God convicts you to look away from something—listen to him.

God, help me to be more in tune with what is good and what is bad for my mind. I want to be wise about what I take in because I know that it will influence what comes out.

COMPARING

Oh, don't worry; we wouldn't dare say that we are as wonderful as these other men who tell you how important they are! But they are only comparing themselves with each other, using themselves as the standard of measurement. How ignorant!

2 CORINTHIANS 10:12 NLT

Do you compare your life to other people's? It's pretty easy to do—especially when you scroll through social media and see everyone's pictures of their friends, their vacations, their pretty hair, and the long string of comments on their photos.

Whether or not life looks good on your Instagram profile doesn't matter much in the grand scheme of things. When you look on social media, you're only seeing highlights of what's really going on in someone else's world. No matter how perfect their pictures look or how many followers they have, they still have the same ups and downs in life that you have. They deal with the same insecurities and have many of the same imperfections. Don't fall into the cycle of comparing yourself with others. It will only make you dissatisfied.

Jesus, teach me to be thankful for the life I have instead of wanting the life someone else has. You have created me to be who I am, where I live, with the body have. I praise you for how you've chosen to make me.

POSITIONS OF AUTHORITY

Everyone must submit to governing authorities. For all authority comes from God, and those in positions of authority have been placed there by God.

ROMANS 13:1 NLT

None of us like being told what to do. We want to be in charge of ourselves—free to decide what we do and how we do it. It seems like there is a natural desire inside us to rebel against authority.

Submitting ourselves to human leadership trains our hearts to submit to God. Do you want to be used by God? God can't use someone that isn't willing to obey him without question. Do you want to live a life that's led by his Spirit and rewarded with his blessing? Then practice now by obeying the leaders that God has put in your life. Your parents, teachers, youth pastor, mentors—they have been put in your life for a specific reason. You will miss out on some incredible relationships and some very valuable wisdom if you resist their leadership.

Dear heavenly Father, you know that it's not always easy for me to obey the people in authority over me. Please help me to humble myself and to trust those you've placed over me.

HOW TO TREAT OTHERS

Do nothing from selfish ambition or conceit, but in humility count others more significant than yourselves.

PHILIPPIANS 2:3 ESV

This statement can be hard one to swallow. What does it mean to think others are more significant than we are? We naturally look out for our own interests. We get hungry, we feed ourselves; we get thirsty, we grab a drink; we are bored, we turn on the TV.

What this verse is saying is that before you meet your own needs, you should be looking to meet the needs of others. Pretend there's only one piece of pizza left, and you're still hungry. The natural first instinct is to grab the piece and eat it. What this verse says is that you might offer that slice of pizza to your friend before grabbing it for yourself. This might be a silly example, but it has big implications. Treat others more highly than you treat yourself.

God, help me to notice the needs of others. I don't want to be so focused on my own desires that I miss out on a chance to help someone else.

REJOICE IN THIS DAY

This is the day that the Lord has made;
let us rejoice and be glad in it.

PSALM 118:24 NRSV

Today, this day, is a gift from God. Think back in your life for a moment. What were you doing two hundred years ago? Can you remember? Absolutely nothing. You had never seen the sun, you'd never known love or friendship, you'd never breathed in the winter air, you'd never laughed. You didn't know about any of these things because you didn't exist.

You aren't guaranteed any more days, either. No one is promised a tomorrow. Your life is precious, and every single day is a gift from God. Rejoice and be glad that God has made and given you this day. Take time right now and thank him for it. Then go out, and make the most of the day you've been given.

Lord, I don't know what today will bring, but one thing I do know is that I am thankful for it. You have given me a wonderful gift by giving me today. Thank you for creating me. You didn't have to make me, and yet you did. I will rejoice in this day.

LOVE WITH ACTION

If someone says, "I love God," and hates his brother, he is a liar; for the one who does not love his brother whom he has seen, cannot love God whom he has not seen.

1 JOHN 4:20 NASB

You can say you love someone, but how much does that really mean if you don't show it? Love without action is nothing. God is love. Not love for those who love him back, or those who are easy to love—just simple, no-strings-attached love.

You can say that you love God, but if you aren't expressing that by loving the people he created, then it means nothing. If you want to love God well, then act it out by loving his people. Loving means setting aside your own needs for someone else. It means being kind, even when you don't feel like it. It means helping someone when you just want to look out for yourself. It means being patient when you've already lost your temper. If you can't love the people around you, then how can you truly love God who is so much less tangible to you? Practice living a life of love with action.

Help me to love everyone, Lord. Give me your heart for everyone around me.

UNSELFISH & CONSIDERATE

Let everyone see that you are unselfish and considerate in all you do. Remember that the Lord is coming soon.

PHILIPPIANS 4:5 TLB

Can we honestly say that we're unselfish and considerate in everything we do? That's a pretty high standard to shoot for. It's our natural human nature to look out for ourselves first. And let's face it, we can get pretty irritated with other people. The last thing we want to do sometimes is be considerate.

God is reminding us of something in this verse—Jesus is coming back soon. Our little annoyances or preferences matter little in light of the grander scheme of eternity. No matter how justified we feel in treating someone less than best, what matters most is how we prepare the way for the coming of the Lord. Are we living out the purposes of Christ on the earth? Or are we just seeking ways to elevate ourselves?

Question your motives and ask God for help to live your best life for him.

God, I want to be ready for your coming. Help me to live a life that will bring you honor and prepare the way for you to come back.

ENJOYING RULES

I enjoy living by your rules
as people enjoy great riches.

PSALM 119:14 NCV

It feels a little odd to be talking about liking rules. Our natural response to rules is normally something closer to frustration than enjoyment. The psalmist recognized the rich benefits of obedience in his life. He realized that by obeying the Lord, he would actually live a better life. A life that was as enjoyable as luxury is to a rich person.

The human heart is easily deceived. We're tempted to be sidetracked in a million directions by pursuing all kinds of things. By staying within the guidelines and rules set out by God in his Word, we can trust that our hearts are being led in the best possible direction. Our own simple act of obedience will lead to a life of fulfillment and wealth in him.

God, I give my heart to you. I commit to following your boundaries for my life. Help me to learn to enjoy obedience. Give me an excitement to follow your rules and to recognize my own richness in your plan.

THE FUTURE AWAITS YOU

I am about to do something new. See, I have already begun! Do you not see it? I will make a pathway through the wilderness. I will create rivers in the dry wasteland.

ISAIAH 43:19 NLT

Take a moment to reflect upon the unique way God has made you and how that has expressed itself through your own educational choices and your personal desires for the future. It isn't always clear to see this, but many of the things you enjoy are actual expressions of God's good plan for your life.

Don't undervalue your joys: they can be seeds of potential that God has planted in the soil of your heart. Jesus has made great changes in you, graduate, and he is making a new thing happen even now.

This is a great reason to rejoice! If God is with you, he has gone before you. Jesus wants you to succeed in the plans he has for you. Allow this blessing to rest in your heart today as you ask him for guidance for the future.

Father, thank you for doing a new thing in me with regard to my circumstances. I see the future for me is much better because of my education. I praise you for your goodness and ask you to help me take full advantage of the opportunities before me.

EMPOWER WITH HUMILITY

"As you wish that others would do to you, do so to them."
LUKE 6:31 ESV

Congratulations! Your hard work has earned you the status of "graduate."

Now, gratefully consider those who did not enter or succeed at this same education. All levels of intelligence and skills are found along the education spectrum. Yet, not all who are conferred degrees recognize or accept this. Are non-graduates berated by your colleagues? In Christ's wisdom you know to not join in their foolish behavior.

God sees, and is pleased with, your upright and kind attitude toward others. You give a good example of Jesus' heart for others when you give respect to all people, regardless of educational advantage. Your kindness opens doors for God to work through people with more limited earthly endorsements.

Father, thank you for giving me an opportunity to be educated and to take a stand of love for those who are not so fortunate as to have obtained my level of education. Please help me to remember that I am no more or less worthy than people of higher or lower levels of education. Put into perspective, for me, the way you view education. That way, I will see it as a tool, and a sweet offering for you.

YOUR DESTINY IS TO SHINE

"In the same way, let your good deeds shine out for all to see, so that everyone will praise your heavenly Father."

MATTHEW 5:16 NLT

As a student, you have focused on coursework, and many other valid interests had to be put on hold. Studies precluded recreation, travel, and even jobs. Graduation changes all that, however. You now have more free time than you have had in many years.

How will you spend this newly gained time?

Consider the possibility that God wants to meet you in new opportunities. Choose to pay forward on your blessings while you also free up time for quiet, friendships, and fun. Share the kingdom of God through kindness and good choices. Your opportunity to put love into action is a beautiful gift of God to you and others.

Jesus, thank you for this opportunity to glorify you. Help me to see where the earth can use a touch of heaven, and let me be that touch.

THE INVITATION

"Behold, I stand at the door and knock. If anyone hears my voice and opens the door, I will come in to him and eat with him, and he with me."

REVELATION 3:20 ESV

Wherever you are, whether you are a day old born again daughter or a seasoned veteran of the faith, walking in all the fruits of the Spirit, this is for you. It is an invitation to go to the next level.

In this verse, Jesus speaks to the church. He plainly tells us that he is ready—right now—to be received by us. What is he talking about? He's talking about us pursuing a truly deep and meaningful relationship with him: the living person of Jesus Christ.

And this is not just an acquaintance-type relationship but a mutual sharing, as we feast upon his presence and do life together. In choosing to open that door and feast with Jesus each and every morning and throughout the day, you will surely taste and see that the Lord is good!

Father, the world is a busy place with a lot of distractions. Help me keep my mind open and my heart attentive to your knock and your voice as you call me to your banquet table. I long to feast with you each day.

THE WISDOM OF PEACE

It is to one's honor to avoid strife,
but every fool is quick to quarrel.

PROVERBS 20:3 NIV

Have you ever just boiled inside, trying to refrain from giving a person a piece of your mind? Good job using self-control! Even though you may hold a key to help that person through his or her troubles, you have used wisdom in not pressing buttons when confrontation is likely. God is like that, too. He is prudent and wise and manages not to pick fights even with the grumpiest of people, or those who are out of sorts.

God is always wise and kind, and the Holy Spirit is affable toward others. Your prayer time with him proves it. When you meet Jesus in prayer, he generates peace in your heart, doesn't he? He often renders a solution in your brain and spreads a smile upon your face as well. These are good outcomes, and they are purveyed to you by the wisest and most intelligent being in existence, God himself.

You are fashioned in God's form. This means you are wired to behave as he does. You aren't designed to dive into disputes and quarrels. The wisdom of God is meant to flow through your life and give you the resources that help you make choices to quell turmoil.

God, there are times I find excuses to quarrel. Your proverbs teach me wisdom, so I would like to learn wisdom from you. Please help me to understand and embody your wisdom as I read through the book of Proverbs. I want to carry peace in my heart and live it out in my life.

LEARNING THROUGH OPPOSITION

Those who disregard discipline despise themselves,
but the one who heeds correction gains understanding.

PROVERBS 15:32 NIV

When given instruction or correction, we thoughtfully glean what betters us. Sometimes we struggle, though, such as when the instructor is antagonistic toward us. This is natural, and no one is immune to it.

Even Jesus had detractors. He is the one and only being who truly understands how you feel and recognizes the disparity between the situation and what it should be.

Jesus' love for you is greater than any situation. He doesn't take notes on what others think and judge you accordingly. Jesus chooses your identity, and that verdict stands. Rest in this so Jesus can protect your heart from pain and pride. Then, you will be able to reap the full benefit of each lesson offered you, even if it is offered in a less than stellar fashion.

Jesus, who do you say I am? Please help me to feel your great love for me. Help me to understand how you are present in times of instruction and reproof. Keep me grounded in the truth so I do not feel assailed when I can be making great gains in self-transformation. Help me to integrate all of what you hold valuable and release the rest to you, so it is no longer my burden to carry. Thank you for your truth and your love.

SACRIFICE OF PRAISE

Through Jesus, therefore, let us continually offer to God a sacrifice of praise—the fruit of lips that openly profess his name.

HEBREWS 13:15 NIV

God is good: really, really good! He advocates for you, and he wants you to bear much fruit.

Sometimes in life, we are faced with challenges that threaten to take our eyes off the goodness of Jesus. If everything in life went well at all times, we would easily be able to thank and praise him, and our gratitude lists would be unending. But in the seasons when life seems unfair or circumstances are far from optimal, it takes more to muster up a sacrifice of praise.

As you praise Jesus, you change the atmosphere around you. The posture of your heart also improves as Jesus' presence permeates your environment. You will begin to start feeling thankful for what you have and can do. As you gain a new appreciation for our Lord in each trail you face, your faith will grow deeper and richer. And if you can learn gratitude in every season, your joyful heart will grow to meet and overtake your challenges.

Father, let there always be a sacrifice of praise on my lips and thankfulness in my heart. I want to always give you praise, regardless of circumstance. I am confident you will overcome, through or for me, in my circumstances. I give you all the glory!

CHOOSE WISELY

Whoever walks with the wise becomes wise,
but the companion of fools will suffer harm.

PROVERBS 13:20 ESV

It's important to choose your friends wisely. If you choose a group of people who are always talking about sex, drugs, and other things they've done wrong, you'll eventually get caught up in their lifestyle—or at least brought down by it. On the other hand, if you choose a group of Christian friends who have set standards for themselves and keep them, they'll only help you in your walk with God.

We learn from those we spend time with. Are you interested in photography? Hang out with someone who is good with a camera. Do you want to be successful in business? Find someone who already is. You will learn from the people you spend the most time with. Make sure those you're investing your time in are passing on things that you want to adopt.

God, help me choose my friends and my influences wisely. I want to better myself, not be brought down.

EVERLASTING LOVE

"I have loved you with an everlasting love;
I have drawn you with unfailing kindness."

JEREMIAH 31:3 NIV

Because we are human, it can be really hard to think of God's love in any other way but how we know it with other people. And with other people, it can often feel like there are strings attached. If you let someone down, if you don't live up to their expectations, you may see them start to slip away or reject you.

Though we may find this hard to believe, rejection is never the case with the Lord's love. It is unconditional. There is nothing you can do to make him turn away from you. He designed you before you were ever a wisp of your mother's imagination, and there are no strings attached to his love.

Father God, thank you for loving me unconditionally. Help me to believe that there are no strings attached to your everlasting love. I am so grateful for my relationship with you.

REMAIN CONNECTED

You must remain faithful to what you have been taught from the beginning. If you do, you will remain in fellowship with the Son and with the Father.

1 JOHN 2:24 NLT

Remember how it felt when you first came to know God? Every word in the Bible jumped out at you. Every story about God made your heart feel something—connected to his love. Fight to keep that connection. The world will try to rob you of it. Sin will try to come between you and God, and the devil will try to make you think that your relationship with him is ruined. Busyness will try to keep you from spending time in his presence, threatening to disconnect you from his love.

People will tell you that being a Christian isn't the best choice. They'll tell you that God's love isn't tolerant. That his Son died for nothing. But fight to stay faithful. Keep the truth always in your heart. Press in to the presence of God and sing his praises until the words of his greatness are louder than the words of your doubt.

God, I always want to stay connected to your love. I don't want to lose my relationship with you because I allowed myself to disconnect. I need you as much now as I did when I first came to you for salvation.

REAL BEAUTY

Those who look to him are radiant;
their faces are never covered with shame.

PSALM 34:5 NIV

Picture a woman on the biggest day of her life—her wedding day. She's radiant and absolutely glows. She is beautiful, every girl's dream. We're told all our lives that inner beauty is what counts, but let's be honest. We really, really want the outer kind—and we're not entirely sure that's ok.

Think about beautiful things—sunsets, flowers, fall leaves. How do they make you feel? Happy, joyful, peaceful? The most beautiful people are those you just want to be around because they make you good.

While there's nothing wrong with wanting physical beauty, beauty that radiates from within is what makes people want to be with you. That kind of beauty is entirely attainable. The more you turn to God, the more you reflect him. The joy, kindness, humility, and peace that come from knowing Jesus radiates from within you—you glow. You are beautiful.

Lord God, I want to be beautiful. I want my eyes to reflect your light and my laugh to reflect your joy. I want my smile to draw others to me, so that I can point them to you.

LEAN IN

With your help I can attack an army.
With God's help I can jump over a wall.

PSALM 18:29 NCV

Scriptures like the one above remind us of the limitless capability of God. Things that are truly impossible on our own (can *you* face an army or leap a wall?) are possible with God's help. This is incredible news, very encouraging, and often misunderstood.

All things are not guaranteed or even probable; they are *possible*. What cannot happen without the Lord *could* happen with his help. But the God of the universe doesn't always intervene. Imagine the chaos if he did! Forty girls, no matter how hard they pray, can't all get the lead in the musical. That test you didn't study for? That's on you. God makes possible the assignments *he* gives you; he helps with the dreams *he* plants in your heart. The closer you walk with him, the more you'll see him work in your life, so lean in.

Lord, I'm leaning in. Align my heart with yours, so all my dreams are from you. Show me which battles to face, which walls to jump. I want to walk with you and watch you work.

UNHINDERED LOVE

"If you love only those who love you, what reward is there for that? Even corrupt tax collectors do that much."

MATTHEW 5:46 NLT

It is natural to love those who show us love. It is supernatural to take the love Jesus gives and spill it upon others who don't reciprocate our love.

Jesus will love you no matter what. Accept this. You are going to be sufficiently loved, regardless of how people feel. When this gets inside you, you will love the unlovable.

Rejoice because your reward in heaven is great because you love others. You glorify God. Jesus is reliable and will walk with you on your journey of love. He has a whole host of people who need your love, and some of them are people you won't expect. Go for it!

God, thank you for loving me in my own imperfections. Thank you for giving me more than enough love, even now, to impact the world around me. I am precious to you. Water the dry parts of my heart and make me a vessel that waters dry hearts, as well.

SEPTEMBER

Be on guard. Stand firm in the faith.

Be courageous. Be strong.

And do everything with love.

1 Corinthians 16:13-14 NLT

BETTER INVESTMENTS

How much better to get wisdom than gold!
To get understanding is to be chosen rather than silver.

PROVERBS 16:16 ESV

Among the first things people consider upon graduation is how to build wealth for retirement and major life purchases. We research the best investment companies, build our strategies, and work our plans, tweaking as necessary for optimal growth. Jesus expects us to provide for ourselves and create financial security.

This is important, and we know it. We need to keep in mind, however, that being financially responsible is only one part of living a wise and insightful life as a believer.

Proverbs provides concise, clear instruction on wisdom. Money is only one topic wisdom addresses. Although caring for yourself and other people through wealth is crucial, wisdom makes the value of riches pale by comparison.

Lord, please help me to have a wise and understanding heart. As I read the words of Proverbs, I want to understand what you have to say and how it applies to my life. You want me to seek the riches of your wisdom and understanding without setting aside your command to work and care for others and myself. Please help me to be wise and have a great perspective on this.

UNSTOPPABLE GOD

"I am the Lord, the God of all the peoples of the world. Is anything too hard for me?"

JEREMIAH 32:27 NLT

You have this book in your hand because you have reached your graduation day. Good job pushing through to your goal! As you look back at your school years, consider what it took to get where you are now. Plenty of people didn't make it. But you did, and it wasn't an effortless task, no matter how people have portrayed it. You did a lot. And you had very good help.

Who do you think helped get you there? A parent or guardian, perhaps? Teachers and administrators working with you in classrooms and behind the scenes? Friends and peers? Jesus? The nudge of the Holy Spirit to learn or remember texts or paradigms? The blessing of God, who ordained you to desire this good outcome, knitting you together as an infant and then guiding and cherishing you in love? Today is a great day to look to the future, gratefully considering the past.

You have an unstoppable God, for whom all things are possible. In step with him, your future will become a fulfillment of his good plans for your life.

God, thank you for being there with me throughout my education. I just want to stop and tell you how very grateful I am to you. You have surrounded me with your love and given me a future that is good. Bless me, and walk with me into this future. I am confident that, wherever you lead me, I will go and be at peace. The future is a beautiful place with you in it.

259

REAP A GOOD HARVEST

A good man is guided by his honesty;
the evil man is destroyed by his dishonesty.

PROVERBS 11:3 TLB

When the farmer plants his crops in the spring, he always reaps the harvest of exactly what type of seeds he has sown. If he plants corn, he reaps corn, often reaping far more than a hundredfold of what he has sown. This can be said of many kinds of seeds.

If we sow the seeds of righteousness, we will receive righteous rewards. When we sow love, we will reap love. If anyone sows the seeds of wickedness or lawlessness, he or she will not reap a harvest of righteousness or obedience but will receive the end product of what has been sown. We are of Christ. Let us always, then, choose to sow what produces heavenly rewards.

If you want good fruit, sow good seeds!

Father, in Jesus' name, I ask you to help me sow good seed, so I may reap a harvest of righteousness and other good fruit. If I am ever lacking in any area of my life, please remind me to sow seeds in that area so I may reap the bountiful harvest that you desire. I thank and praise you.

JUST BE THERE

They sat down with him on the ground seven days and seven nights, and no one spoke a word to him, for they saw that his grief was very great.

JOB 2:13 NKJV

When someone is going through a tragedy, we don't always know what to do. We're used to passing out opinions and encouragement, so we may think we have to say something in order to be helpful. It can be tempting to repeat old clichés, like, "Everything happens for a reason," and, "God doesn't give us more than we can handle."

Here's another option. Tell the truth. Tell them you're sorry, and you have no idea what to say. Rather than trying to fix the situation, just be there. If you read the book of Job, you'll see that his friends got a lot of things wrong, but this one they got right. When they saw at first how great his sorrow was, no one said a word.

Father God, your Word is amazing. Everything I need to know about love is contained in its pages. Today I learned that sometimes the best thing to say is nothing. Thank you for this wisdom, and may I remember it when the time comes.

ENTIRELY LOVELY

The Lord said to Samuel, "Do not consider his appearance or his height, for I have rejected him. The Lord does not look at the things people look at. People look at the outward appearance, but the Lord looks at the heart."

1 SAMUEL 16:7 NIV

A 2001 movie featured a character hypnotized so he would see people as attractive or unattractive depending on what kind of people they were, rather than on what physical beauty they had. As a result, he fell deeply in love with a woman he never would have looked at twice. The film was heart-warming, thought-provoking…and completely unrealistic.

Spend five minutes in nature, and you'll see that God is as in love with beautiful things as anyone. After all, he gave us our sense of beauty. He wants his creation to be enjoyed. However, when it comes to people, appearance is not his first priority—and he doesn't want it to be ours. More than anything, the Lord cares about our hearts.

Father, examine my heart and show me how to be more beautiful in your eyes. I want to be lovely to you.

WHO DO YOU LOVE?

Dear children, let us not love with words or speech but with actions and in truth.

1 JOHN 3:18 NIV

"He says he likes me on the phone, but when I see him in the halls he acts like he doesn't even know me. It's so confusing." Sound familiar? Few things are more puzzling than a person whose actions don't match their words. A parent can say, "I love you," every day as they leave the house. If they roll their eyes, ignore us when we talk, or never choose to spend time with us, we're left wondering. Do they really?

Jesus taught that love is about what we do, and he modeled this with his ministry. He didn't tell the sick people, "Oh, I feel so bad for you! Get well soon!" He healed them. He didn't say, "Oh, no food? Bummer!" He fed them. Who do you love, and how do they know?

Lord, I don't want anyone to wonder if my love is for real. Inspire me to help, to encourage, and to pour myself into my relationships. Help me love not just with my words but with my whole life.

HOW DOES YOUR GARDEN GROW?

The entire law is fulfilled in keeping this one command:
"Love your neighbor as yourself." If you bite and devour
each other, watch out or you will be destroyed by each other.

GALATIANS 5:15 NIV

Girls fight, right? Even if you manage to stay mostly out of it, someone close to you is probably living this right now. Rather than trying to figure out who is right, let's be encouraged by this verse to choose peace. It's a powerful image. Picturing our arguments as bites out of one another, we can easily see the danger—eventually, there will be nothing left.

Considered less graphically, imagine a garden. Your fights are flowers torn from the ground, and your forgiveness and grace are new plantings. At the end of the season which area of the garden will be lovelier? Where will you more easily sense God's presence?

Lord, you love peace because you love us. You want what's best for us, and you know that fighting and disagreements tear us apart and kill our roots. Forgiveness and grace allow us to flourish and grow and be more aware of your presence and love. Help me remember this, God, so I can continue to grow closer to you.

TO KNOW HIS DAUGHTER

Is anyone among you suffering? Let him pray.
Is anyone cheerful? Let him sing psalms.

JAMES 5:13 NKJV

How is your prayer life? Perhaps you recite memorized prayers. Or maybe you find yourself blurting out your needs and asking for help as they arise or thanking him for blessings large and small when you recognize them. Maybe you have a journal filled with letters to the Father. All of these are equally pleasing to God, provided you are coming to him with an open heart and focused mind.

Prayer is simply talking with God. As many ways as there are to converse, there are ways to pray. He wants to know how you feel about him, what you're sorry for, what you're grateful for, and what you need. He wants to know what you fear, what you dream, and what you wonder about. Like a good and loving father, he wants to know his daughter.

Father God, when I think of all the people in the world, I'm amazed that you are so interested in me. You long for my love, you forgive my sins, you shower me with blessings and you help me with my needs. How can this be, and how can I thank you?

GOD WANTS TO UPGRADE YOUR THOUGHT LIFE

Let the words of my mouth and the meditation of my heart
be acceptable in your sight,
O Lord, my rock and my redeemer.

PSALM 19:14, ESV

Have you ever wished you could take back words after you had spoken them? Most of us have. Although the frequency of these indiscretions seems to decrease as we gain wisdom, the weight of our words increases a great deal over time. Simply put, we learn over a lifetime just how much words matter.

You are entering a new season of life, graduate. How will you use your two strong resources of cognition and expression? Post-graduation is a crucial time to consider how your thoughts and words affect your life and others.

Present them all to Jesus, and choose to keep those thought and speech patterns that glorify him, leaving the rest in your past.

Father, please give me new thoughts to replace anything useless that I have allowed in my mind. In place of negativity give me enlightenment. In place of discouragement give me your zealous hope. If I start to say something neither kind nor helpful, prompt my spirit to stop before I hurt others or myself. Thank you for caring about the way my thoughts and words impact others.

CHRIST WILL RECONCILE

Draw near to God, and he will draw near to you.

JAMES 4:8 ESV

When somebody holds a grudge against you, his or her first inclination isn't to run up to you as you approach him or her. He or she is not looking for a hug!

However, Jesus says that no matter where you are on the spectrum of faithfulness, he isn't looking for you to make everything right before you approach him. He wants you to come to him with an open heart and all your foibles. He isn't interested in grudges, but in reconciliation, responsiveness, and redemption.

Drop off every hindrance and run to him! He is the one who justifies, and he is the one who heals. Even right now. He is ready to draw you nearer than you have been before, and make your life wholesome wherever it has lacked. In Christ, you lack nothing.

Thank you, Jesus, for this new day on the earth. There have been areas of my heart I have been afraid to go. There are places I am ashamed of. Please forgive me and draw near to me as I draw near to you. You have promised you would, and I know you do not lie. I want the warmth of your heart embracing my own. Please give me renewed fervor and a wholesome, upright heart. I love you, Lord Jesus.

PATIENT WITH PATIENCE

Let patience have its perfect work, that you may be perfect and complete, lacking nothing.

JAMES 1:4 NKJV

It would be so good to be perfect in everything we lack, wouldn't it? We would never risk hurting others or looking foolish. We wouldn't be flawed in our manners or conduct. We would create good wherever we went. It sounds so good! Why can we not have this as our constant reality?

Although we do fret over our insecurities, Jesus is completely able to handle our situation. He isn't promising to go against our wills to make us perfect outside our desire to improve. But he doesn't sit up and wring his hands over us each time we slip up or make an unwise or unloving choice. Rather, he walks into our lives when we invite him and makes changes, as we are ready to adopt them. He is gentle and kind, and he is slow to anger, patient with our weaknesses, and faithful to the process.

Would we rather have anything different?

Jesus, you are so kind. Thank you for your compassionate friendship and your guidance through the process of our redemption. You are kind and gentle, and I love you. Because you are patient with me, I'd like to become patient with myself, too. I will also be patient with others, knowing how you transform my heart as you touch it. Thank you for your blessed goodness.

SIMPLE BUT CONSUMING

"Return to your home, and declare how much God has done for you." So he went away, proclaiming throughout the city how much Jesus had done for him.

LUKE 8:39 NRSV

It sounds like the last thing Jesus told us to do, doesn't it? His cry might sound like this: "Go tell people! Go tell them how good I am, how I love you, and how I heal you where you need it."

At the end of life, who would not appreciate knowing who Jesus is and what he could have done for them? Nobody. So everyone is fair game.

Tell the good news. Let people know you are grateful. You aren't selling a bill of goods; you are telling people where their help comes from. Don't delay in telling people the truth of why you are so very happy: it's Jesus, Jesus of Nazareth. He is 100 percent good, 100 percent kind, and 100 percent interested in the life of each person on the planet. Nobody ever has to be alone. Let this good thing consume you.

Jesus, thank you for your salvation. Show me who you want me to tell about your love. Tell me for whom to pray and give me an open heart to share in ways that bless the people around me. Help me to be sensitive to the Holy Spirit, sensitive to your heart, and sensitive to the needs of people that I really want to reach. I promise to listen and try to walk with you in obeying your command.

CHRIST'S PERSPECTIVE MAKES VICTORY POSSIBLE

Jesus looked at them and said, "With man this is impossible, but with God all things are possible."

MATTHEW 19:26 NIV

We all experience life's problems. In the midst of these tumultuous times, we strain to see our way through or beyond the troubles before us. We look upward at our mountain and cannot even fathom to see its end through the clouds.

The Lord wants to change our perspective so we will look at our problems from a different angle. If you are born again, you are a new creation. You are in Christ, and he is in you. Jesus sits at the right hand of God the Father, so now your new perspective comes from a heavenly view, which makes the problem seem smaller.

God is completely for you, and he wants to partner with you in dealing with anything that comes against you. He is the one who split the sea in half so Moses and the Israelites could walk through. He is the one who has raised the dead and who performs endless miracles for all of us. The world cannot contain them any better than all of creation could contain the glory of God. From this perspective one can see the truth: with God, nothing is impossible.

Father, when I face life's problems and feel overwhelmed, please remind me of who you are. All things are possible with you. Remind me of your heavenly perspective on the issues at hand, reminding me that you have them covered and you will walk me through them.

THROUGH THE STORM

"Anyone who listens to my teaching and follows it is wise, like a person who builds a house on solid rock. Though the rain comes in torrents and the floodwaters rise and the winds beat against that house, it won't collapse because it is built on bedrock."

MATTHEW 7:24-25 NLT

Everyone loves a good story. And Jesus was a master storyteller. In this parable, two people built different houses. One house was built on sand and the other on rock. When rain poured down, floods rose, and the winds whipped up around the house built on rock, the house stood firm. When the rain poured down on the house built on sand, the house collapsed. Neither home was exempt from the storm.

Precious one, even as a child of God—even as a *wise* child of God—you'll experience storms. The temptation is to blame yourself or say, "Why is this happening to me? I must have done something wrong." Good and bad things happen to everyone. What's different is God's presence and peace in the storm. You don't need to be afraid. Call on the name of Jesus, and he will give you the stability you need when all else is shaking.

Father, thanks for the promise of your presence even in the storms of life. Help me build my foundation on you, my rock, so when storms come, I don't need to be afraid.

WHAT ARE YOU EATING?

I could not address you as people who live by the Spirit but as people who are still worldly—mere infants in Christ. I gave you milk, not solid food, for you were not yet ready for it. Indeed, you are still not ready.

1 CORINTHIANS 3:1-2 NIV

When a baby is born, he or she can only eat one thing—milk. No burritos, no steak, no smoothies, no potatoes. Just milk. But as babies gets older and their digestive systems mature, they can begin to enjoy other foods, like corn on the cob, or chef salad, or a big piece of pizza. Those foods make them grow and thrive. If they tried to live on just milk, they wouldn't have enough energy to get through the day.

This is the analogy Paul makes. He calls the adult Christians "infants." That's not a compliment. He wishes they were more mature. Instead they are still drinking milk.

What are you eating? Are you able to chew on the difficult areas of following Jesus and obey, receive his loving discipline, and give him all you have? Or are you like an infant who can't handle all that a mature Christian can? God isn't looking for instant maturity, but he does want commitment to taking steps in that direction.

Jesus, I want to be a mature Christian, someone who isn't caught up in small, worldly things. Help me to dig deep into your Word, to know you well, and to be open to correction.

IN THE LOVE OF GOD

Keep yourselves in God's love as you wait for the mercy of our Lord Jesus Christ to bring you to eternal life.

JUDE 1:21 NIV

How frustrated do you feel when you tell people something and they refuse to believe you. That's how God feels when he tells you he loves you and you question him. "If God really loved me, then this bad thing wouldn't have happened," you might say. Or, "God says he loves me but I've messed up so badly."

Despite what you might think, God loves you deeply. And he knows that his love is intended to be your very lifeblood. Knowing God loves you will be the primary force that sustains you through rejection, suffering, and loneliness. His love is perfect. It isn't manipulative or self-serving, but pure. You also play a part in this great love. You can choose to reject it or accept it. God tells you to remain in his love, wanting you to have all the benefits it brings. Don't run from it.

God, help me to believe in the depth and height and greatness of your love for me. When you discipline me, help me remember that you are doing it for my own good. Your love never fails.

HIGH QUALITY

God demonstrates his own love for us in this: While we were still sinners, Christ died for us.

ROMANS 5:8 NIV

The difference between a Coach purse and a knock-off at the local mall is quality and cost. A Coach purse has a high cost that comes with prestige. Because of that cost, it's highly valued by the person who bought it.

You were bought at an extremely high cost. That's proof of God's love. God loved you so much he sent Jesus to die on the cross so you could have forever life. It's also proof of your value to God. He wouldn't have paid such a high price if he didn't think you were worth it. God chose you. He wanted you as his child. He was willing to initiate the relationship with you and pay whatever price it took to ensure that you had the opportunity to become a daughter in his kingdom.

Father, thank you that you were willing to pay the price for me to enter your kingdom.. Thank you for valuing me and loving me.

ATTACKED

We are not fighting against flesh-and-blood enemies, but against evil rulers and authorities of the unseen world, against mighty powers in this dark world, and against evil spirits in the heavenly places. Therefore, put on every piece of God's armor.

EPHESIANS 6:12-13 NLT

Sometimes you are doing everything you can to obey God, and you still feel like you are getting hit from all sides. This is because we do not just wrestle with flesh and blood. Satan and his demons do have power and influence on the earth. When sin entered the world, it brought disorder where there was once peace.

While that is a fact, it shouldn't scare you. God has given you instructions on what to do when you feel attacked. James 4:7 says first to submit yourself to God. That's right. Don't proudly try to solve your own problem: submit to him. Then resist him and he has to flee! Not because you are great but because God's Spirit lives inside you and *he* is great.

Praise you, God, that victory is yours. You've promised that, as your daughter, I can resist the devil and he has to flee. There is no one as strong, powerful, and mighty as you who fights for me.

A PERFECT PLAN

The Lord makes firm the steps of the one
who delights in him.

PSALM 37:23 NIV

There are certain privileges that come with being a daughter of the King. Namely, you will live forever in his kingdom. Another privilege is having the opportunity to find out the perfect plan God has for your life. You simply don't have the big picture that God does. You don't see all that he sees or know what he knows. So any steps you plan to take are limited by what you know and what you see.

Because God though is aware of everything and knows you intimately, he is capable of leading you into a beautiful plan. Humility says, "God, I know you know me better than I know myself, so I choose your plan for my life." If you follow his lead, the Lord will make your steps certain and firm.

Father, thank you that I am yours. I want to humble myself before you, knowing that it's a decision I'll never regret.

JESUS ANSWERS MY CRY

I was in trouble, so I called to the Lord.
The Lord answered me and set me free.

PSALM 118:5 NCV

Jesus so dwells within the praises of his people that we may reliably count upon him to make himself felt and known by calling upon him, worshiping him, and praising him when we are troubled.

When life throws a curveball, run to the holy place. Our songs of worship and declarations of praise are medicine for our souls. They bring us into God's presence, where our pains are extracted from our souls and we are strengthened within our spirits and souls. In fact, solutions to problems are often revealed in moments of worship and praise. Let us give our Lord praise every single day as we revel in his goodness and love.

God will show himself to whomever he chooses. Let us draw near and experience his grace and freedom where we are.

Praise you, Jesus! Thank you for your love and mercy. You are divine in nature. You are kind and humble. Your goodness knows no end and your compassion elevates us from our circumstance. I praise you in your holiness and give you the honor you are due.

FRESH START

If anyone is in Christ, he is a new creation; old things have passed away; behold, all things have become new.

2 CORINTHIANS 5:17 NKJV

When you asked Jesus to redeem you from your old life, he forgave your sins and set you on a new path. On that new path, you have hope and peace, and God himself is your constant companion. You are never alone, and you are never without hope. Why, then, does it sometime feel like you need a fresh start?

As a part of human nature, we find that two parts of us war within. Sometimes, our choices are not good. Other times, we are wearied by toil or impacted by others' actions. Life can be hard. But you have not been built for the short run. No, you are built for the expanse of eternity, and Jesus is the one who is going to see you through. Be true in your faith, as he is true to you.

The Bible clearly states that God's mercies are new every morning. That means there is a "sell by" date on your troubles. Ask Jesus to lighten your load by lifting off your burdens that you are not to take. You are, after all, a new creation. Even your worries must submit to the authority of Jesus.

Jesus, thank you for forgiving my sins and giving me a new start when I ask. I renew my faith in you and submit myself to your leadership. Please remove from me whatever is not pleasing to you. Help me to be refreshed each morning in the newness of your grace.

WHOLE HEART

If you look for me wholeheartedly, you will find me.

JEREMIAH 29:13 NLT

You must search with God for your whole heart because he wants your whole heart. Jesus doesn't want half of your schedule or the part of you that isn't put off by obedience. He wants exactly as much of you as he allowed of himself to hang on the tree: 100 percent, all of him and everything.

To call Jesus God and not give him all of you would be to say he's a great advisor, but that you can exist outside of his sphere. It simply isn't true. And you will miss out on so much more of Jesus than you ever banked for if you hesitate in giving him everything.

Jesus is the kindest, most loving person you could ever meet. He knows everything about you—and he cares for everything about you. That is why he speaks to you in countless ways, beckoning you nearer. He wants you to experience love in its fullest, even now, as his child. You will never stop getting to know him in this lifetime. There is always a way to dive deeper into his sea of love, and there is always, always more of him to know.

Jesus, refresh my love of you. Refresh my hunger and my drive to seek you with my whole heart. Let's go on an adventure together: an adventure into the relationship of you and me. I want to see you clearly and understand your heart. All of me needs you.

A REMINDER TO HOLINESS

"Get rid of all moral filth and the evil that is so prevalent and humbly accept the word planted in you, which can save you."

JAMES 1:21 NIV

James wrote this sobering message to the twelve tribes of Israel. It wasn't that they were not saved or that they didn't care about Jesus or others; they really did. It's just that there are times we make choices we know are not best.

After a while, these choices accrue spiritual interest, and we can lose our way in the faith. May God forbid that this happens! But this warning is written plainly in the Bible, so we are warned to keep watch.

James went straight to the heart of the point: people were quick to gloss over what they thought they knew. They would interject with their opinions when being told something that might help them, and they were glad to grab onto the grace Jesus offers without holding firm to the holiness he expects. James' adjuration to choose to live an upright life and to cleave to what the Bible says is a verse that clings to our hearts and offers life even this day.

Father, you have a plan for my life. Please help me to clear away activities and attitudes that do not glorify you. I want to read your Word and do it, so I can be your child who stands before you without fear, knowing I have nothing to regret at the end of my days. Watch over me to perform your will in my life.

THE GREATEST LOVE

Greater love has no one than this,
that one lay down his life for his friends.

JOHN 15:13 NASB

What is more desirable than Christ's love? It is wholesome, other-driven and all consuming. Nothing in you that is lacking survives in the fire of Christ's love. This dross from our lives drips off of us and is no longer able to affect our lives. We are freer than we have ever been.

In order to give us this love in an expressible and useful way, Jesus came to the earth and acted it out on the stage of life before all mankind. He then died and arose to drive away the sting of death from the lives of anyone willing. This is the God you serve! Hallelujah!

Jesus calls you his friend. He doesn't like you because you are now "clean." He loves you—flat out, unabashedly loves you—and made you clean so you could experience that love. Oh, the enormity of his grace and love! Jesus calls you his friend. He lets you in on his life and his plans, and he calls you forward to overcome, a victor regardless of what it cost him to crown you. This is great news given by a great friend.

Thank you, Jesus, for calling me a friend. I will always have you! Thank you for deciding to make my life wildly fruitful. You are good. I am so grateful for your friendship. Please walk with me, as a friend, in your special way, today. I look forward to a day of discovery and joy, abiding in you.

DOING GOOD FOR MY NEIGHBOR

Each of us should please our neighbors for their good, to build them up.

ROMANS 15:2 NIV

The Roman church had a hot, fiery love for Jesus and his church, too. They loved people dearly, but they lived in a fallen world much like we do. In fact, these Roman Christians lived in a city that persecuted them. It was a dog eat dog world out there, just as it seems to be in our own modern times, now and again.

So, if your neighbor takes advantage of you, it isn't that you have done something wrong. Give that to Jesus; do not let it weigh your heart down! Let the Holy Spirit show you what good your neighbor needs—go by the Holy Spirit's prompting and not by your own understanding. Now, go out and fulfill that need in whatever way you are led. Do not hesitate to obey God in doing good.

If you are stumped as to what you should do, read the rest of Romans 15, and see what might jog your thoughts as to what nice turn you may do for others. Jesus loves you; love others with the love he gave you.

Holy Spirit, you have loved me well, and you want me to love others for their own sakes. Show me people and opportunities to serve people according to their own good. I love and trust you in this.

GOD HAS YOUR BACK

Oh, don't worry; we wouldn't dare say that we are as
wonderful as these other men who tell you how important
they are! But they are only comparing themselves with each
other, using themselves as the standard of measurement.
How ignorant!

2 CORINTHIANS 10:12 NLT

It is refreshing to see that Saul, too, had to fight for his job
at least one time! It is not uncommon to fight now and then
for your status or your job—to put in the "over and above"
effort to prove you are exactly where you belong. Do not fear
the battle, and do not even fear the defeat. Rather, fear the
Lord who has put you in this place for such a time as this.

Let everything you do glorify God by improving your
employer's bottom line and interests and by blessing the
coworkers that you have around you.

You could be planted in a work situation for a lifetime or
for several years, but the fact remains that your usefulness at
your position should never be under question. And if it ever is
. . . fight for it. Your job is a gift of God to you and those you
impact through your work.

God, please help me to bless you in all that I do. I know you
have given me this opportunity to work. If conflict or other
factors find their way toward me, I ask you to back me up
and show me how to work in my boss's best interest at
work—and to bless you and glorify you in everything.

THE ABIDING ONE TRANSFORMS ME

Jesus Christ is the same yesterday, today, and forever.

HEBREWS 13:8 NKJV

Have you ever decided to study something very deeply only to find you have reached the same conclusion that you had in the beginning?

Jesus is like this! He literally never changes. The more you encounter Jesus, the more you realize he is holy, worthy, good, and kind. Jesus showers love, honor, and goodness upon your soul as you abide in him. It is his great joy to bring you into a full understanding of all you possess at the very moment you choose him. We know this is a gift we unwrap over a lifetime: he is eternally expansive in his exquisite goodness. Yet, he never changes.

When you study God's word and seek Jesus face to face, you will not find a variance. Rather, you will find yourself changing into the likeness of Christ, in all his beauty and glory. He rejoices to glorify himself within and through you. He always has.

Jesus, please help me understand you through the reading of your Word and time spent in prayer. Transform me to your image according to your will.

OPEN THE WORD TO LEARN

The unfolding of your words gives light;
it gives understanding to the simple.

PSALM 119:130 NIV

You might think of your school years as being years of studying, but the truth is that you are constantly learning. One of the areas where the most dynamic learning will always take place is in the realm of learning Scripture. It is true that we read one book, the Bible. But we never really grasp all that this guidebook for life has for us while we are still on the earth. Why is this?

The Bible says that it is living and breathing. That doesn't mean it needs fresh air and good nutrition! It means your Bible, as it sits on the shelf, waits for you to open it at any time and get from it live-giving wisdom that will help you in your world *today*.

You do not need to read the entire Bible each day to get adequate insight. Study your Bible well, however, with the help of the Holy Spirit, so it is always fresh on your mind. Then, when you are in a position where you need God's wisdom, his Word can speak into your heart without you having to search for an answer for God's will.

Father, I am going to read my Bible. Help me to grasp what you are trying to say to me in your Word, and show me the ways it might apply to my life. Will you please help me to be a diligent reader of your Word? I believe I will glorify you better as my mind is renewed through regularly reading the Bible.

285

GOD IS ENTHRONED ABOVE LEADERSHIP

Everyone must submit to governing authorities.
For all authority comes from God, and those in
positions of authority have been placed there by God.

ROMANS 13:1 NLT

It is a mark of maturity and courage to step forward and support unsavory leadership at work or in government. Do you have the character and patience to be fruitful and productive in a system under the name of one who does not have your personal approval?

It hurts to feel betrayed or unrepresented by your workplace or government. We want to feel represented and cared for. Today, we must each take this verse as seriously as the Christians did in the early church days. Ask Jesus how to pray for and be supportive of your leadership and your structure, whether it is business or government. The God of all consolation is with you. Trust him to be beside you. He holds leadership responsible just as he holds you responsible.

Keep this in mind for personal peace: you work for God, and he is Lord over all. You are, therefore, in good hands, and what he wants to do in an organization is greater than whose name gets to be on the head plaque for a term.

Lord, I am glad that you are Lord of all. I am grateful that you have your hand on leadership and that all you want of me is to trust you and obey. I ask you to bless those in leadership over me and to do your will in their lives and in the areas they touch.

PRAISE JESUS IN ALL THINGS

I was naked when I was born, and I will be naked when I die.
The Lord gave these things to me, and he has taken them away.
Praise the name of the Lord.

JOB 1:21 NCV

When Job cried out this mournful praise, he had lost much in his life. Job was attacked by two foreign nations and two forces of nature in one day. His children were destroyed, his servants were slain, and his livestock were slaughtered. One of his children's homes was demolished as well. Yet praise was on Job's lips.

When we praise Jesus, we invoke his name and request his presence. This is the most powerful thing we can do in any situation. Even if the Lord doesn't answer us as we hope, we must understand that our trying to deduce why things happen isn't going to win us a personal victory.

When we look at Job, we know instinctively that this is the right answer for us. Let us praise the name of Jesus, our Lord, who has brought us into the world with nothing and will return us to himself in the same manner. This Lord is the author of our faith.

What have I been given that was not from you? What will I take with me that I have accrued on the earth? My life is a short moment in the span of all time, and you have carried—and will carry—me through to the end of the days you have apportioned for me. Let me be faithful to you, then, Lord, in all my days, whether they are dark or bright. I praise you, Jesus.

OCTOBER

Let the beauty of the Lord
our God be upon us,

And establish the work of
our hands for us.

PSALM 90:17 NKJV

YOUR GIFTS ARE GOOD

Every good and perfect gift is from above, coming down from the Father of the heavenly lights, who does not change like shifting shadows.

JAMES 1:17 NIV

Do you doubt yourself as you enter a new place in the work world? Are you worried about what kind of employer will want you or how well you will do in the new job you are getting after your graduation?

Quit doubting. God knew what he was doing when he made you, fashioning your interests and loves. He gives you the godly desires of your heart, and who you are can be a great asset to the right employer.

Jesus is your beginning and end. He has chosen the gifts that he has put into your life, and he will give you opportunities to give the strengths of your gifts for the best interests of his kingdom and the economy in which you live. Trust your instinct on this: you are valuable, and Christ in you will help unlock your good and perfect gifts.

Father, thank you for giving me an identity as a valuable person, and thank you for choosing only good gifts for me. Help me to bring these gifts into all areas of my life, including work. I know you will go with me; you have promised to never forsake me. Help me to thank you by shining your light at work and being the employee you desire me to be.

WHAT TO WEAR?

"Seek the Kingdom of God above all else, and live righteously, and he will give you everything you need."

MATTHEW 6:33 NLT

If you have a date or are going to a prom or a wedding—even just arriving on the first day of school—you've probably thought a lot about what you were going to wear. Believe it or not, God knows you like to look good.

Jesus said, "Look at the lilies of the field and how they grow. They don't work or make their clothing, yet Solomon in all his glory was not dressed as beautifully as they are. And if God cares so wonderfully for wildflowers that are here today and thrown into the fire tomorrow, he will certainly care for you" (Matthew 6:28-29). Solomon was the king of Israel. You can be sure that he had a closet full of clothes.

Worrying about clothes, worrying about what people think of your clothes, and spending too much time and money on them are signs that they've become too important. What's most important is seeking God and living right. If you do that, he'll take care of the clothes part of life.

Father, help me to set my eyes and my heart on more important things than what I wear. Please remind me to seek your kingdom first.

FULL LIFE

"The thief comes only to steal and kill and destroy;
I have come that they may have life,"
and have it to the full."

JOHN 10:10 NIV

Have you ever had a supposed "friend" who said and did all the right things while around you but behind your back was completely different? Our enemy, the devil, is a lot like that. He's a two-faced liar whose ulterior motive is to steal, kill, and destroy. He sets out to destroy lives and relationships, steal peace and joy, and kill any chance of people enjoying a sweet relationship with God.

Jesus Christ, on the other hand, longs to give life—*full* life. Where the enemy steals, kills, and destroys, Jesus gives, builds up, and encourages. He brings courage, joy, peace, and a sense of confidence.

God, thank you for the life you give. Help me be alert to anything that isn't from you.

STREAM OF GRACE

O Lord, you are so good,
so ready to forgive,
so full of unfailing love
for all who ask for your help.

PSALM 86:5 NLT

The Bible teaches that we have all sinned. There is not one believer in all of creation that has never sinned before God. Jesus is the only perfect man to have ever walked the earth. He alone bears the title of being the sinless one.

Because we have all sinned, we are in need of cleansing. God readily offers his forgiveness the moment one of his children cry out in repentance. He happily pours on a steady stream of grace and healing to the repentant heart. Sometimes, even after we have repented of certain sins, we still don't *feel* clean. But God wants you to know that no matter the extent your sin, upon your confession to him, he will make you clean. He is good and ready to forgive.

Father, thank you that your words have the power to make me clean after I have sinned. Please heal me and help me to walk closely to you so that I might hear your cleansing voice whisper, "You are clean."

FATHER OF LIES

*"There is no truth in him. When he lies, it is consistent with
his character; for he is a liar and the father of lies."*

JOHN 8:44 NLT

Satan hates God with a fierceness that we can scarcely
comprehend. Because of this, his favorite thing to do is
to wreak as much havoc as he possibly can. Jesus is not
intimidated by this. He teaches us how we should navigate
Satan's actions on the earth. Satan is incapable of ever speaking
the truth. He is the original source and the father of lies.

This is precisely why you have to closely watch your
thoughts. Not every thought that flies through your mind is
from you or God. Some are whispered by Satan. You don't
need to fear though. As you grow in discernment and maturity,
you will be able to realize that those negative thoughts are not
coming from you. And if you know that, you don't have to feel
guilty or dirty. Simply call on the name of Jesus, and invite him
to help you take every thought captive and make it obedient
to him. He will give you the grace to resist Satan's lies.

**Father, thank you that your Spirit of truth is alive in me and
will give me the strength I need to resist lies when they
enter my mind.**

REWARDS

*Anyone who comes to him must believe that he exists
and that he rewards those who earnestly seek him.*

HEBREWS 11:6 NIV

Our culture loves rewards. As children, we are often
introduced to reward systems. It's very simple. The giver of
the rewards makes it clear what needs to be done to earn the
reward. Often, there is a correlation between the difficulty
of what is being asked and the size of the reward. The more
difficult the task, the greater the reward.

We love this system because we were made for it. Our
Father in heaven loves rewarding his children. He sees every
single act of obedience that we make toward him, and he
knows exactly how much effort we put forth in obeying
him. This delights his heart, and he loves demonstrating his
pleasure through rewards. Some of his rewards will be given
to us on earth, but many are being stored up for us in heaven.
Don't doubt this truth.

**Father, thank you for your rewards. Give me long-term
vision to serve you well, knowing that you are watching
and rewarding my efforts.**

HEARING THE TRUTH

"When the Spirit of truth comes,
he will guide you into all truth."

JOHN 16:13 NLT

Do you have a steady habit of hearing truth? It's important to form that habit for a few reasons. It will give you wisdom where you lack it, freedom where you feel stuck, and peace where there is fear. The world will not speak truth to you. It will tell you you're ugly when you're beautiful, urge you to hold a grudge instead of forgive, and call "good" the things that are evil.

When you have a regular diet of hearing truth, you become quicker at discerning Satan's lies before they seep into your mind and heart. From free Bible audio apps, to worship music, to online sermons, you really have a buffet of options for hearing truth. Make the choice to put truth in your heart daily. You won't regret it.

Father, give me the strength to pursue hearing truth
regularly at the expense of other habits.

PUTTING OTHERS FIRST

Do nothing from selfish ambition or conceit, but in humility count others more significant than yourselves.

PHILIPPIANS 2:3 ESV

God says we are all made in his image and likeness. This means we all bear the image of God the Father, Son, and Holy Spirit, and we are most in our element when we act in a godly fashion, even in the midst of a fallen world. That is how powerful God is . . . and that is how much faith he has in you to recognize who he is and to flourish under his loving care.

As image bearers, we Christians exemplify our maturity by acting in love and honor toward others. When we are motivated by love, we cannot go wrong because love never fails. As we foster love and honor for others, all people are enabled to flourish.

In dealing with people from various walks of life, we do not need to stand in agreement with incorrect viewpoints or lifestyles in order to love and honor them. Instead, we come from a place of humility and add value to them, regardless of where they are in life. Let us allow Jesus to show us the way as we walk in step with him.

Father, thank you for creating me to be your image bearer. Thank you for giving me your example, through Christ, of how to hold others in honor and love so I may live in peace. Please help me to be mindful of your presence and how I portray you as your image bearer.

GOD HELPS US GAIN OUR INHERITANCE

Whatever you do, work at it with all your heart, as working for the Lord, not for human masters, since you know that you will receive an inheritance from the Lord as a reward. It is the Lord Christ you are serving.

COLOSSIANS 3:23-24 NIV

Because you are actually working for the Lord regardless of your vocation, you have every right to ask Jesus how he wants your day and its activities to play out. Take a moment now or at the beginning of an activity, to ask the Holy Spirit what he would like to see happen with what you are doing. You can ask him the purpose of your work, the methods you should use, or even if the activity should be done at all (we know time wasters are not usually good for business, for example). Regardless, you will find there is a biblical basis for the way God does things, and it reflects his good, holy, and kind nature.

At the end of each day, thank the Holy Spirit for spending the day with you, helping you to become productive and well motivated. You will end the day with peace and renewed vision for the next shift. Knowing God's ways will give you fresh insight in how to work well, and it will also bolster your enthusiasm for the job you hold.

Lord, I have not always had healthy attitudes about work. Sometimes, I need help doing it well. Will you please be with me in a special way, today, and help me to be the best employee I can be? I would like to work hard and do well for my boss and my corporation. Most of all, I want you to be very proud of me.

297

THE RICHNESS OF RULES

I enjoy living by your rules
as people enjoy great riches.

PSALM 119:14 NCV

A game is only fun if everybody plays by the rules. Open up a Scrabble® box and the first thing you see are instructions on how to play the game. First and foremost, any combination of tiles must form an actual word, as found in an English dictionary. So, go ahead and make a big play with *sesquioxidizing* but try to lay down *daqszxite* and it won't fly. Making up your own rules as you go along causes confusion and frustration for the other players. It also increases the probability of tiles flying across the room.

Rules aren't meant to squelch our fun or limit our enjoyment. A few boundaries actually increase our sense of security and keep us from losing our way.

God's rules for living, as found in Scripture, provide us with some much needed protection in a world where it seems like anything goes. The less we quizzify (419 points) God's rules, the more we'll realize he's not trying to highjack (374 points) our fun.

Lord, thank you for giving us good guidelines and directions. Forgive us for resisting your commands. Help us to find joy in following the path you mark out for us.

EVERY HAPPY MOMENT

God wants all people to eat and drink and be happy in their work, which are gifts from God.

ECCLESIASTES 3:13 NCV

Your heavenly Father wants you to enjoy your life. Not just the big moments of life, but the everyday ones—the eating, hanging out, working ones. Look for him in the simple pleasure of breakfast with a busy parent, lunchtime laughter with a table full of friends, the study date where that science formula suddenly makes sense, band and basketball practice… He is there, watching and waiting for your delight.

Every happy moment is a gift. It's easy to forget this, especially when frustrations demand so much of our attention. Take a little time today to slow down and notice the everyday blessings God gives you.

Father God, thank you for my sweet little life. I confess to rushing right past the gifts of time with people I love, good food, and the hobbies and pastimes that make me, me. Help me to sense your presence in the laughter of friends, a snuggle with a pet, and the million other ways you choose to delight me.

GOD IS FOREVER

We do not look at the things which are seen, but at the things which are not seen. For the things which are seen are temporary, but the things which are not seen are eternal.

2 CORINTHIANS 4:18 NKJV

Have you ever been so angry with a friend you thought you might never forgive her, only to realize a few days later you're enjoying each other again? Or felt as though your heart was broken beyond repair, only to laugh about it a few weeks later, wondering how you could have possibly been that sad over something (or someone) so silly?

One of the things your heavenly Father wants you to understand is that from his perspective, everything here on earth will eventually seem like that broken heart—temporary. God is forever. That's how long he has loved you and how long he will keep on loving you.

Father God, on the days the things I can see are too much for me to bear, help me remember all the beautiful, unseen things you have planned for me. Remind me that I am your beloved daughter, today and forever.

KNOWN FOR WHAT?

"Don't judge others, and you will not be judged. Don't accuse others of being guilty, and you will not be accused of being guilty. Forgive, and you will be forgiven."

LUKE 6:37 NCV

Have you ever been wrong? Of course you have. We all have. You make a decision and within moments you know you shouldn't have done it. You say something, and the second it leaves your mouth you know you shouldn't have said it.

While you may have made poor choices, you didn't become a bad person. You became a person in need of compassion, forgiveness, and grace. When someone says or does something wrong, quickly trade places with them in your heart so you can give them the same understanding you'd want them to give you. Be the kind of person who is known for compassion, forgiveness, and grace so that when you need it (and you will!), it will be given to you.

Perfect Lord, I confess to judging people based on their choices, though I'd never want someone to judge me that way. Help me to see others as you see them. I want to be known as you are, for grace, forgiveness, and endless compassion.

JUST BECAUSE

From his fullness we have all received, grace upon grace.
JOHN 1:16 ESV

Don't you love "just because" gifts? No holiday, no achievement, no birthday, just a gift—just because. Whether it was store bought gift, a heartfelt letter, or unasked-for favor, it has the same, wonderful effect. A gift you weren't expecting or don't deserve makes you feel particularly special.

These unmerited, "just-because" offerings are a perfect illustration of God's grace. We all are welcome to the undeserved forgiveness offered through Jesus' sacrifice on the cross. On top of that, each and every day God shows us grace for our mistakes, blesses us, and involves himself in our concerns. We don't earn it; in fact, we don't deserve it at all. Just because he loves us, just because he delights in us, just because he feels like it, the Lord heaps grace on top of grace. Who can you surprise with grace today?

Jesus I will never get over what you did for us—for me—when you sacrificed your life for all my sins. I don't deserve your grace, but just because you love me, you give it again and again. Thank you.

MORE LIKE YOU

Whoever has this world's goods, and sees his brother in need, and shuts up his heart from him, how does the love of God abide in him?

1 JOHN 3:17 NKJV

When we're little, our understanding of the Bible is fairly contained. God made the world. Noah built a huge boat and took the animals on a trip. Jesus loves me. If I pray and ask him into my heart, I will go to heaven. Then we grow up, and encounter verses like the one above. They make us uncomfortable.

The truth is, God sometimes wants us to be uncomfortable. In this case, uncomfortable enough to be bothered because someone else is in need. He wants us to care more about others than ourselves. Because we are human, this is difficult. So what do we do? Recognize how far we have to go—how far we will always have to go—and ask him, "What can I do today to grow more like you?"

Lord, I have so much, yet sharing is hard. I even find myself wanting more. I realize how generous and perfect your heart is, and how desperately I need your love to live in me. Teach me how to love like you.

PATIENCE OVER POWER

Better to be patient than powerful;
better to have self-control than to conquer a city.

PROVERBS 16:32 NLT

Read the verse again, and think about it for a few moments. Do you believe what it's saying? How might patience be better than power?

Jesus' ministry sheds a brilliant light. Think about who Jesus was. He was God—in the flesh! Being God, did he have to *walk around* for three whole years talking to and healing small groups of people? Couldn't he just tap into all that power and transport himself and the disciples wherever he wanted to go? While we're thinking about it, couldn't he just have forced everyone to obey him?

Of course he could have done all these things and more. Yet Jesus chose patience over power, self-control over conquering. Why? Because he wants friends, not slaves. God wants to know us, not to own us, and relationships take time.

Lord, I don't always want to learn to be patient. I just want to be there already. Thank you for Jesus' example. Life with you is about relationships, and relationships require patience. Thank you, too, for your patience with me.

THE REAL FIGHT

Our fight is not against people on earth but against
the rulers and authorities and the powers of this world's
darkness, against the spiritual powers of evil in the
heavenly world.

EPHESIANS 6:12 NCV

When we call a company's customer service department
to register a complaint, most likely the person answering
the phone is not the one responsible for our problem. Yet,
that person on the other line usually gets the brunt of our
frustration. It's not fair to vent our dissatisfaction on that poor
employee. Their job is to recognize the root of the issue and
bring resolution, while maintaining a positive attitude. Our job
is to extend some grace to the person trying their best to deal
with our complaint.

Conflict in our relationships has less to do with people
than we think.

We need to recognize that there are spiritual forces at work
causing hostility and divisiveness among us. Instead of fighting
with our brothers and sisters, we need to take the fight where
it belongs—to the devil and the powers of evil in the world.

Lord, help us to see the underlying causes of conflict in
our lives. Forgive us for battling with people who we tend
to think of as the problem. Give us insight into the real
issues and help us stand against the devil's schemes.

AND THE WINNER IS

It wasn't their swords that took the land.
It wasn't their power that gave them victory.
But it was your great power and strength.
You were with them because you loved them.

PSALM 44:3 NCV

When an actor wins an Academy Award, the ensuing speech is usually laced with long lists of people's names that deserve some recognition. The music begins playing in the background, but it doesn't matter. Credit needs to be given where credit is due, because no one can reach that level of success by themselves. The person holding the Oscar is keenly aware that many others contributed to this moment of glory.

Sometimes we're tempted to take credit for our own successes. We may attribute our good grades to our exceptional intellect. We might bask in our athletic achievements or expert skills on the job.

It's important to remember that our abilities come from God. Our gifts and talents are tools from our creator, but it is his strength and power that give them life.

Lord, thank you for your steadfast love that sticks with us whether we succeed or fail. Help us to develop our abilities so that you can use us to make a difference in the world. We will give you all the glory.

SPARROWS AND HAIRS

"Are not five sparrows sold for two pennies? Yet not one of them is forgotten in God's sight. But even the hairs of your head are all counted. Do not be afraid; you are of more value than many sparrows."

LUKE 12:6-7 NRSV

Do the math. If five sparrows sell for two cents, then each bird is worth four one-thousandths of a penny. Considering that there are thirty-five species of sparrows, there must be millions of these little birds in the world. Yet, God hasn't forgotten even one. The average person has 150,000 hairs on their head, but who's counting? Apparently, God is.

What could be more insignificant than sparrows? Why does it matter how many hairs we have? Is God trying to tell us something?

Most of us want to make a difference in this world. We want to find a career path, discover our calling and contribute in a meaningful way. Until these things become clear, we often have to battle a fear of failure and feelings of insignificance. God is saying, "Don't worry. I've got you."

Lord, it's amazing that you care about every single detail of our lives. There is nothing that is hidden from your eyes. Help us to see that you valued us enough to send Jesus to die in our place.

NO WORRIES

When anxiety was great within me
your consolation brought me joy.

PSALM 94:19 NIV

What are you anxious about today? Sometimes we know exactly what is causing the uneasiness in our souls, and sometimes it's hard to pin down. That jittery feeling might stem from a buildup of outside stress or from inner pressure to perform. It could be a result of strained relationships or financial worries. Anxiety often creeps in when we're fearful of something looming in the future.

What do we need when we're overwhelmed and unable to squelch those panicky thoughts racing through our minds? We need someone to come alongside us and calm us down. We need a voice to speak truth into our situation and help us gain perspective. We need a friend who will divert our attention from our troubles and make us laugh.

The writer of this verse was dealing with great anxiety. So he turned to God. The fact that the psalmist wrote about his anxiety in the past tense tells us that the joy of the Lord brought him out of his despair. What are you anxious about today? Tell God all about it.

Lord, we tend to let things build up until it almost seems unbearable. Remind us to come to you with our worries, big and small. Ease our burdens and lift our spirits when fear wants to pull us down. Thank you for being our faithful friend.

ROCK OF AGES

Don't just listen to God's word. You must do what it says.
Otherwise, you are only fooling yourselves.

JAMES 1:22 NLT

Have you ever gone rock climbing? It takes a lot of skill to master the techniques needed to scale a sheer rock face. Learning about the sport is one thing—being a rock climber is another. You could watch hours of videos and observe live demonstrations of professional climbers. You could buy the best equipment and subscribe to climbing magazines. You could download rock-climbing playlists and join a rock-climbing club. With all that valuable information, you could fool yourself into thinking that you are a real rock climber.

Knowing and doing are two different things.

It's possible to listen to God's Word and stop right there. Putting what we hear into action is the crucial next step. We'll never know the thrill of living an authentic life of faith until we test the harness of God's promises, trust the rope of his faithfulness, and dig our hands and feet into the true rock, Jesus.

Lord, I want to know you and not just know about you. Give me a clear understanding of what it means to live a Christian life. Help me to step out and experience the thrill of a life wholly committed to doing what your Word says.

THE BEST IS YET TO COME

"Things which eye has not seen and ear has not heard,
And which have not entered the heart of man,
All that God has prepared for those who love Him."

1 CORINTHIANS 2:9 NASB

A knock on the door announcing unexpected company can strike fear into the heart. In a matter of seconds, dirty clothes get stuffed under the bed, clutter on the counter is swept into a bag and thrown into a closet, and a candle is lit to cover up the smell of last night's pizza. Knowing ahead of time that company is coming give us a chance to make special plans for our guests. And it gives us time to clean the bathroom.

God is anticipating the day we get to join him in eternity, and he is going all-out to get ready. What will we see? Perhaps colors beyond our ability to imagine, or flowers and trees never dreamed of before. What will we hear? Possibly some musical instruments never conceived, or the singing of heavenly beings. As amazing as this seems, the very best thing our eyes will see is Jesus' face. And the richest sound will be the voice of the God saying, "Well done! Come on in and share my happiness!"

He's getting ready for this day. Are you?

Lord, our hearts can't begin to grasp what's in store for us. Thank you for preparing a place for us in your heavenly kingdom.

310

BUILDING PLANS

Unless the Lord builds the house,
the builders labor in vain.
Unless the Lord watches over the city,
the guards stand watch in vain.

PSALM 127:1 NIV

Have you ever stayed up all night working on an assignment for school or a project for work and then realize in the morning that you did it all wrong? Far from being lazy, you worked hard for hours, and you put your best effort into its completion. But when you become aware that all your labor has been for nothing, discouragement sets in. It's hard to find motivation to pick up and start over again.

No one sets out to fail. We work hard with the intention of doing well and making a good life. But when we leave God out of our plans, it's like constructing a house without a foundation.

Whether we are building a career, a business, or a relationship, all of our best efforts will be in vain without the firm foundation of Christ. When we seek him first, the exhausting chase is replaced by a life driven by meaningful purpose. What he builds, lasts.

Lord, we ask you to be the center of our lives. Help us to look first to you for guidance and direction as we make plans for our future. Reveal your will so we can follow your lead.

IN THE ZONE

*Set your minds on things that are above,
not on things that are on earth.*

COLOSSIANS 3:2 NRSV

Years ago, people used to set their watches by the sun. In the modern age, Greenwich Mean Time was the standard used for regulating the time. And now, atomic clocks keep perfect time on our cell phones. We can't call the U. S. Naval Observatory and tell them to set the atomic clock according to our wishes. We adjust to their standard.

In order to set our minds on things above, we need to consciously align ourselves with God's way of thinking. By reading and studying his Word, regularly meeting with other believers, and exposing ourselves to sound biblical teaching, we can begin to have an eternal perspective that rises above the trends that come and go in our culture.

This world wants to convince us that money, social status, toys, degrees, and promotions are the measure of a life. But we don't need to adjust to that current of thought. Let's set our hearts and minds on God and stay in his zone.

Lord, we often feel the pressure to conform to what the world says is right and wrong. Help us not to get caught up in the ever-changing cultural trends and stay steady with the truth of your Word.

EYE TO EYE

Give me your heart.
May your eyes take delight in following my ways.

PROVERBS 23:26 NLT

When a mother is trying to get her toddler's attention, she might say, "Sweetie, look at me when I'm talking to you." She knows that if she can get that child to look up at her, there's a better chance her instruction will get through. If a dad is trying to get the truth out of his teenager, he might say, "Son, look me in the eye and answer me." He knows that it's easier to hide something when avoiding eye contact.

When God asks for your heart, he's saying, "I want your full attention." But he doesn't demand it like a commanding officer barking orders to his soldiers. He's not a dictator pouring out threats or a manipulator putting a guilt trip on you.

This is an invitation to take a good look at him. Trust him with the deepest part of you, your heart.

Lord, my heart is prone to wander. There are distractions that pull me away from you, and there are times I avoid you because I am ashamed of my sin. I don't want to hold back from you anymore. Please take my heart and fill it with your love so I can delight in following your ways.

STAY OUT IN THE OPEN

*Have nothing to do with the fruitless deeds of darkness,
but rather expose them. It is shameful even to mention
what the disobedient do in secret.*

EPHESIANS 5:11-12 NIV

Never has it been so easy to engage in private, questionable behaviors at anytime anywhere. Electronic devices and the Internet bring helpful information right into your hands, along with wasteful and woeful pursuits and enticing images at the touch of a finger swipe. Ask yourself some serious questions:

In your current online activity, would you be comfortable being observed by your parent or boss?

Does this endeavor add to your health and well being? Your work achievements?

Are you avoiding more important tasks? Why?

What does God think about your deeds done in private?

Do you need some accountability to help you stay out in the open? Who could you ask?

No matter what you have experienced or struggled with online in the past, you can do better. The digital world is not going away. Figure out how you can access it publicly, proudly, and productively.

**Dear God, help me to live in the open with my electronics
and private activities. Give me the courage to do what is
right, even when no one is looking.**

MOVING AND SHAKING

"Truly I tell you, if you say to this mountain, 'Be taken up and thrown into the sea,' and if you do not doubt in your heart, but believe that what you say will come to pass, it will be done for you."

MARK 11:23 NRSV

Driving into Colorado brings the anticipation of the breathtaking Rockies. In any season, the towering peaks offer splendor in floral display or glittering whiteness.

At this transition time in your life, you may be facing many mountains. The job search seems impossible. After the campus freedoms of daily schedule choices, you find yourself back at home or living with others who make demands on your time. Friendships take a lot more effort than at school. Money is not pouring in, but the debts and bills are in full view.

How can you move the mountains? What about the fear that you will fail? Your knees are shaking as you try to climb each hill. God says believe in him, not yourself. Spend time with him. He is the original mountain-maker and can guide you to the top.

Creator God, my mountains seem overwhelming at times. Show me how to move them one stone at a time and conquer my fears. Thank you that I can depend on you.

FINDING FAVOR

When people's lives please the Lord,
even their enemies are at peace with them.

PROVERBS 16:7 NLT

Be kind. Say thank you and please. Smile. Listen longer. These are all simple strategies, yet they are often absent in personal exchanges today. Are they out of style? Ineffective?

Who notices if we practice manners or exhibit politeness?

We should ask God how to respond to others. Current cultural trends reward selfishness, sarcasm, pithy comebacks, and harsh language. If our coworkers, family members, or chance encounters on the elevator find us pleasant, we have the possibility of gaining favor. The investment of assisting a stranger or forgiving a friend might not be paid back immediately, but the continuous application of right living will have a powerful return overall.

Gracious God, help me offer a smile or an open door to people I meet. As I learn about relating rightly to you, I can employ the same principles with others. Thank you for guiding me.

BETTER THAN A GUN

A person without self-control
is like a city with broken-down walls.

PROVERBS 25:28 NLT

What is the best way to protect ourselves? Buy a firearm, obtain a gun permit, and take self-defense classes while learning to shoot the weapon? Install a top-of-the-line security system in our home, add extra locks to the doors, and station a pit bull on guard duty?

Today, as in past decades, many cultures in the world construct walls around a village and individual family's properties. Western neighborhoods with easy access from the street feel too vulnerable to behind-the-wall-dwellers. Do walls protect us?

King Solomon is telling us in this verse that what we urgently need is personal boundaries, self-control, and restraint to find safety and security. Fighting and antagonistic behaviors cause us trouble and compel others to target us for retaliation. When we are at peace with our fellow citizens, we are insulating and protecting our families and ourselves in solid ways.

Jesus, show me how to control my emotions and words and how to live at peace with others. Help me not to let fear and the world's problems take over my daily relationships. I want to trust in your ways.

A GREAT RÉSUMÉ

Know therefore that the LORD your God is God;
he is the faithful God, keeping his covenant of love
to a thousand generations of those who love him
and keep his commandments.

DEUTERONOMY 7:9 NIV

Putting together a quality career résumé can be humbling, especially if you don't have much to report at this stage of your life. You have the diploma, and hopefully, you have engaged in profitable community service or work experiences to demonstrate you can be depended upon to at least show up.

Potential employers want to know what they are investing in if they hire you. Will you follow directions? Respect others' opinions and positions? Follow through with paperwork and deadlines? Make a positive contribution to your new team of colleagues?

When you look at God's record in the Bible, you see he keeps his promises to people, even when they drop their side of the agreement. He shows you how to forgive offenses and think of yourself humbly when approaching those in authority. Toward his people, he gives 100 percent love and effort. Let him be your source of daily security as well as your model of faithfulness to build your personal résumé.

Father, your model of faithfulness is perfect. Thank you for your unending love and care for me. Help me to show dependability to others and earn their trust.

NOT A REALITY SHOW

Do not let anyone treat you as if you are unimportant because you are young. Instead, be an example to the believers with your words, your actions, your love, your faith, and your pure life.

1 TIMOTHY 4:12 NCV

When you watch a steady diet of reality shows as a teenager, what happens? Do you find yourself wanting the attention, the glamour, the luxury, and circumstances of someone else? How does your real body and your real family compare to what is on the screen?

The realities outside the door of your bedroom and inside your bank account show a very different story. Turn off the tall tales of television and focus on you. You have something valuable to offer just like you are, with your imperfect skin and quirky sense of humor and everything.

While figuring out *what you want to be when you grow up*, solidify the *kind* of person you are. Concentrate on the qualities that reflect well in any situation: honesty, kindness, compassion, loyalty, responsibility, humility, generosity, curiosity, optimism, and respect. The world needs to have more people living a real life modeling excellent character than another self-consumed reality show.

Father, help me see that the life I have been given is a great story that you began writing before I was born. My future is what I make it and is very real. Forgive me when I compare myself to others. I want to glorify you and enjoy the person I am becoming.

NOVEMBER

Take delight in the Lord,

and he will give you your heart's desires.

Commit everything you do to the Lord.

Trust him, and he will help you.

PSALM 37:5 NLT

ADORED

"You are a people holy to the Lord your God.
The Lord your God has chosen you to be a people
for his treasured possession, out of all the peoples
who are on the face of the earth."

DEUTERONOMY 7:6 ESV

You are like a precious flower. You are absolutely the apple of your Father's eye. He loves and cherishes you beyond comprehension. Daughter, you are *adored*. When you adore something, you don't just love it; you watch it, protect it, and handle it with great care. Your Father doesn't want to miss a thing. He wants to know every detail of your life. He handles you with such great care because he wants you to fully become who he intended you to be.

Because God adores you, he sometimes allows you to go through some things that don't feel good. But God is perfect. He is good, loving, and protective. You can trust that in those difficult moments, he is shaping and molding you to be more like him.

God, I want to believe that you adore me, and that I am a richer person because of the difficulties you have allowed to cross my path. Thank you for your goodness in those moments and for loving me completely.

SIMPLY DELIGHTED

"The Lord your God in your midst,
The Mighty One, will save;
He will rejoice over you with gladness,
He will quiet you with His love,
He will rejoice over you with singing."

ZEPHANIAH 3:17 NKJV

Did you know that the mighty God, creator of heaven and earth, is a proud Papa? That's right! He is a loving Father who delights in you—his child! He created you not just so you can enjoy him, but so he can enjoy you. Every good thing that is in this world is from God and teaches us about his character. Humor and laughter, art and creativity, peace and quiet, and excitement and surprises: all are a part of who he is. There are many things that he enjoys, but we are at the top of his list.

God delights in the way you see things, the sweet thoughts you have, the things that make you laugh, and the way you represent him. He delights in your hard work and determination. He adores you because he made you. You are his.

Thank you, God, that you love me and nothing can change that. Help me to be encouraged by that today.

THE MEASURE OF SUCCESS

*The plans of the diligent lead to profit
as surely as haste leads to poverty.*

PROVERBS 21:5 NIV

Success is hard to measure. Who is successful? The one who tries her very best and gives it her all? Or the one who puts forth just enough effort to get the job done? Do you ever wonder why you should do things with all of your heart? Why you should finish every single project or assignment well? Why you should even bother?

Nothing good comes out of not trying your best. There's no success or sense of pride and accomplishment. There is no reward in cutting corners. Who wants to be known for their lack of attention to detail, their careless ways, or lazy, half-hearted attempts? Being diligent every day takes a lot of effort and energy. It also takes discipline. But through it all, your character is being shaped and strengthened. Even if the reward isn't immediate, the day will come where you will be able to see the fruit of your labor.

Lord, help me to be diligent in every task even if my efforts go unnoticed. Let my completed work be a reflection of my desire to honor you in all I do.

STRANGLING FEAR

"Be strong and courageous. Do not fear or be in dread of them, for it is the Lord your God who goes with you. He will not leave you or forsake you."

DEUTERONOMY 31:6 ESV

Some people are afraid of spiders, others are afraid of the dark. Fears are not uncommon, but we don't usually like talking about them. Sometimes we don't share our fears because we are embarrassed or because we feel like we will look weak and silly. But if we bottle up our fears, they have the tendency to grow into huge obstacles that are challenging to overcome.

Fear has a way of strangling our hope and courage. It can keep us from living a free and joy-filled life. It can keep us from pursuing our dreams. It can even keep us from making wonderful friendships and experiencing new things. Fears can grip us if we don't give them over to God. God is our light in the scariest of places. With him by our side, we can face whatever causes us to be afraid.

God, I lean on you today and ask for your help. Give me a boldness like I've never known before. I know I can conquer my fears with you at my side.

DEVOTED IN LOVE

Be devoted to one another in love.
Honor one another above yourselves.

ROMANS 12:10 NIV

Your school or neighborhood is probably filled with many kids that come from different walks of life. Some kids have a lot of money, some do not; some are considered "cool" and others not so much. There are kids that have talents that make them popular, while others have important talents that are hardly recognized. Have you noticed who most people choose to be friends with?

When we think about Jesus and his friends, we remember that he befriended the underprivileged, the tax collectors, and the not-so-popular. When these individuals got to know Jesus as a trusted friend, they felt honored and loved for who they were. He honored others above himself. Because of this, their lives were forever changed. It is easy to honor, love, and be friends with those that are like us, but it is Christ-like to look for those who may need a friend and make them feel loved and respected by honoring them above yourself.

Lord, please show me if there are people in my life that I need to give more honor, love, and respect to. I want to be devoted to others in love and start honoring them above myself.

IN AWE OF GRACE

In him we have redemption through his blood,
the forgiveness of sins, in accordance with the
riches of God's grace.

EPHESIANS 1:7 NIV

Have you ever seen anyone at a restaurant insist on paying for a bill twice? Not likely. Nobody in their right mind would pay for a bill that was already paid for in full, would they? It wouldn't make any sense. Yet we all fall into this terrible habit of reminding ourselves of our past mistakes and sins. We allow ourselves to be entrapped in what once was and forget that we are already redeemed. Our sins were already paid for. We are free and clear. Sin free. Debt free.

It doesn't matter who you were or what you did in the past. In God's love for you, in his mercy and grace, not only has he forgiven you, but he has redeemed you from a life of despair. He has taken what was once lost and broken, and transformed it into something beautiful.

Thank you, God, for clearing my history of sin. Help me to walk in freedom from condemnation and guilt. You took all that upon yourself so that I could live a new life. I am in awe of your grace.

SUPERNATURAL STRENGTH

Do you not know? Have you not heard?
The Lord is the everlasting God,
the Creator of the ends of the earth.
He will not grow tired or weary,
and his understanding no one can fathom.
He gives strength to the weary
and increases the power of the weak.
Even youths grow tired and weary,
and young men stumble and fall;
but those who hope in the Lord
will renew their strength.
They will soar on wings like eagles;
they will run and not grow weary,
they will walk and not be faint.

ISAIAH 40:28-31 NIV

No matter how puny your muscles may seem to you, you are stronger than you know. You can do anything you set your mind to. And you'll do it because God gives you a supernatural strength to power through and endure.

God never wearies. He never gets too tired to help you make it through the worst the world can throw at you. Put your hope in him, and he will give you strength beyond your wildest imagination.

God, give me the tenacity to make it through the toughest of times. I know I can because you are with me.

327

WHAT IS PEACE OF MIND WORTH?

A heart at peace gives life to the body,
but envy rots the bones.

PROVERBS 14:30 NIV

"My total collection of clothes fits in half my closet," the college freshman girl tearfully told her mother. "Other girls are storing outfits in my extra space."

"Hey, why don't I ride with you tonight to the fraternity party?" the young man texted to his friend with the new Jeep. He glanced at his own dependable, older model car and sighed.

Envy and discontentment are like a dry throat that can never drink enough to quench the thirst. Constantly wanting more or better eats away from the inside and takes a toll on the body as well as the attitude. Jealousy destroys relationships and blinds the eyes to what treasure is already present.

Contentment is a decision not based on circumstances. We take a clear inventory of our personal possessions and ourselves and determine whether or not we are okay.

Others will have more, and there will be others with less. But this is our life to enjoy. So make peace with your current situation, the worth of who you are and what you have. Don't waste time looking for greener grass.

Generous God, you have given me so much, and I want to let gratitude rule over envy. Help me not to lose my peace of mind through jealousy or discontentment. Thank you.

HOLD MY HAND AND SHOW ME THE WAY

*When you turn to the right or when you turn to the left,
your ears shall hear a word behind you, saying,
"This is the way; walk in it."*

ISAIAH 30:21 NRSV

What is more comforting than a familiar hand gripping yours to show you where to walk or just to communicate companionship on a journey?

You have many roads to travel in the days and years ahead. Let God be your guide through known and unknown areas of your life. Strange, shadowy places quickly prompt you to call out for him to light your way. You might think at other times, *I got this. I know where I'm going.* Watch out. The times we easily run into the ditch or back into a fencepost result from the assumption we don't need God's directions.

When you feel alone, perhaps unsure of the next step or too overwhelmed to figure things out, listen for God's voice. He may speak through the Bible or counsel from a wise friend or circumstances that answer your specific prayer. Trust in his leadership, take hold of his hand, and follow him.

**Father, thank you for your continual guidance in my
life. Help me lean on your wisdom and not my own
understanding. Please hold my hand and lead the way.**

THERE ARE GIANTS ALL AROUND

When I am afraid, I will put my trust in You.
In God, whose word I praise,
In God I have put my trust; I shall not be afraid.
What can mere man do to me?

PSALM 56:3-4 NASB

We love the story of David and Goliath. When the little guy takes down the giant, we cheer. David was experienced with big brothers pulling rank and fierce animals attacking his flocks. He learned how to defend himself with his sling and possessed a determined spirit. Did he put his trust in his muscle and crafty strategies to win against his opponents? No!

The Psalms record that David knew to look to God from a young age. Later as a king and army captain, he continued to recognize that the source of his help came from beyond himself. God made him, and God was in charge. This declaration granted David true security and protection.

Whether the looming danger is loneliness, unemployment, financial stress, health concerns, or global terrorism, you have access to God who knows all about the challenges. Trust in him and face your giant.

God, you are greater than any giant problem. I need to remember you have helped me before and will again. I don't want to be afraid. You are with me. Thank you.

STAND UP AND STAND OUT

I am not ashamed of the gospel, because it is the power of God that brings salvation to everyone who believes: first to the Jew, then to the Gentile.

ROMANS 1:16 NIV

Students from Black Forest Academy appeared on the church stage to give testimonies before entering the baptismal tank. Their stories gave credit to childhood faith as the means to combat high school eating disorders and self-worth issues. A few reported a newfound relationship with Christ that they had never understood until recently.

The final candidate for baptism stepped up to the microphone. A young lady from Iran delivered a vastly different narrative through her translator. For the first time in her life, while living in a refugee camp in Germany, she heard about Jesus in a new way. Her background allowed for no Savior and no Son of God. Now she read the New Testament and fell in love with the God-man who treated men and women equally. She believed he loved her enough to free her from the penalty of sin and offer entrance to heaven. She was ready to live for him.

How will you be challenged to stand up for your faith? There are those around the world willing to give up everything for the freedom Christ offers. Think about your public testimony as you go about your daily life as a Christ-follower.

Thank you for the provision you made for me to have peace, Jesus. Give me courage to stand up for what I believe and even stand alone if required.

A CAKE IS BAKING

We know that all things work together for good to those who love God, to those who are the called according to His purpose.

ROMANS 8:28 NKJV

Somebody is having a birthday, and it's time to put your baking skills to the test. No box of cake mix this time around so out comes the recipe: flour, butter, salt, eggs, baking powder, sugar, milk, and vanilla. How can this possibly turn into something good? The heat activates each ingredient to do its job—the flour becomes the framework, the baking powder provides fluffiness, the sugar sweetens, the milk provides the moisture, and the eggs hold it all together. A wonderful aroma wafts from the oven. And something wonderful is about to emerge!

Your life is kind of like that cake.

Every experience you've had, difficult and delightful, becomes the fabric of who you are. Individual events may seem unimportant, isolated, and pointless; however, when God is the baker, he is able to work everything together for your good and his glory. Every single joy, sorrow, success, and failure is blended together and purified by his love. What is that lovely fragrance? Oh, it's you!

Thank you, Jesus, that you will take all the pieces of my life and make something beautiful! Help me to continue to trust that every detail is being worked out into something good!

THE NEXT CHAPTER

"Look at the new thing I am going to do.
It is already happening. Don't you see it?
I will make a road in the desert
and rivers in the dry land."

ISAIAH 43:19 NCV

Textbooks are shelved. Papers are filed for future reference. Grades and transcripts made their final appearance, measuring the past years of effort, or lack of effort, and setting the record in stone. This chapter of your life is finished.

Graduation celebrations and words of encouragement come from all directions. Talk about future plans and dreams fill the conversations and your nervous thoughts. A new chapter needs to be written.

While you were learning to walk, to read, to ride a bicycle, or to use your first cell phone, God knew this day would come, and he already has words for you on the next page. Ask him about your destiny and seek his guidance and understanding about your preparation to this point. He is making a way for you.

Father, you alone know me and my future. Help me to see the wise path you have been laying before me and how to follow. Help me write a new chapter that brings glory to you and satisfies my heart's desires. Thank you for your care for me.

THE GOLDEN RULE

"Treat others as you want them to treat you."
LUKE 6:31 TLB

The United Nations displays a framed poster, The Golden Rule, in its New York hallway detailing thirteen religious and spiritual traditions that promote this Scripture's peaceful formula for treating fellow human beings. Around the world, the ideal of kindness and respect being reciprocated when practiced crosses cultures and languages. But does it really work?

In truth, you know that you have offered kindness and received unkindness in return. Conversely, maybe a stranger helped you for no known reason. Should you embrace this principle for handling human interactions? What is the alternative? Expect respect when you are insensitive and harsh? Look for friendship, overtures, and invitations when you never extend any yourself?

Trust that God knows what he is prescribing. Believe that kindness and respect toward others will result in positive actions returned. The world knows this rule is correct, and effective.

Dear God, we should honor you by how we treat one another. Thank you for providing a guide for the whole world that can lead to peace and better relationships. Help me to be a vessel of kindness and respect to people in my life. I place my trust in you for the results.

MATCHES AND MIRROR BALLS

"Let your light so shine before men, that they may see your good works and glorify your Father in heaven."

MATTHEW 5:16 NKJV

When the electricity goes out, you reach for a match to light a candle. Such a small thing, not fancy and not often noticed, has the power to dispel the darkness.

Mirror balls attract much more attention with their hundreds of shiny surface pieces, reflecting bits of light around a room in a spinning, random design. You can't count on these flashy fixtures to give you an accurate summary of your surroundings and they depend on light already present to create their glittery display. Which would you rather be? A match or a mirror ball?

In this new season of your life, as you seek to build a reputation for work and future relationships, determine to be a walking source of light and power. Be dependable and available. Be the person called on when clarity or help is needed, not just someone to offer entertainment or decoration. You can add sparkle in time, but you need to radiate consistent light first.

Creative God, help me to focus on reflecting you in my work and relationships. I want to be a dependable source of truth and light in my world. Show me how to shine in the right way and draw people to you through my life.

UNLOCK THE DOOR

"Look! I stand at the door and knock. If you hear my voice and open the door, I will come in, and we will share a meal together as friends."

REVELATION 3:20 NLT

When a locked door separates a parent and child, fear grips the grown-up. What peril is happening on the other side of the door? How can he help if he cannot reach his little one? God, as a loving parent, wants no locked doors between him and his children. When we feel like hiding away, shutting God out of our heart and life, we lose out on the help we need.

When we are expecting a family member or friend, we often leave the front door open.

"Welcome! Come in," the open door says, "We are looking forward to seeing you."

God sent us Jesus, who understands the human need for friendship and promises to come in when we open the door of our lives to him. Through prayer, study of the Bible, and relationships with other Christians, we can learn what friendship with Jesus is all about. We learn how to trust God like Jesus did. Open the door and invite your friend Jesus into your everyday world.

Father, I don't want to shut you out of my life. I need you. Thank you for sending Jesus to be my friend and savior. I want to keep the door to my heart wide open to receive your grace and wisdom.

COUNT TO TEN OR WALK AWAY

Avoiding a fight is a mark of honor;
only fools insist on quarreling.

PROVERBS 20:3 NLT

The freckled-faced sixth grader said, "I can't help it if I have a bad temper. I get mad easily. People need to leave me alone or else I cannot help hitting them." His face was almost as red as his hair. The playground monitor and classroom teacher exchanged glances. They regularly heard such excuses for fighting and settled in for a lengthy discussion with the young man. His parents had supplied lots of monetary goodies but little mentoring for their only child.

Is there a core value that keeps people from fighting, with words or actions? Or is it just a matter of learning coping techniques during times of stress and frustration to avoid fights? Do we gain from fighting? Do we lose when we walk away?

King Solomon, the wisest man who ever lived wrote the verses above, suggesting the best response is to avoid fights. Cultures around the world present anger, violence, killing, and all manner of conflict as the way things work. Wisdom says differently. Ask for help if you enter fight mode. Don't be a fighting fool. There is a better way.

Dear God, you say fighting is for fools. Help me be a person of peace, even when others around me are pushing toward conflict. Give me courage to walk away and be different than the world. Thank you.

RESPECT YOUR ELDERS

Whoever ignores instruction despises himself,
but he who listens to reproof gains intelligence.

PROVERBS 15:32 ESV

Graduates today have some unique expectations for their lives and careers. They want personal fulfillment and purpose in their work, not just a paycheck. They want vast social connections and opportunities to learn new things constantly. Do older generations have any experience to offer that is seen as relevant and helpful?

Mentoring and coaching continue to be rich sources of sharing wisdom and instruction for young adults. Both provide structured feedback and information exchange but in different forms. Mentors offer expertise and knowledge about a particular area of work or activity to guide someone less experienced. Coaches create an environment through challenging questions and accountability for individuals to progress toward self-selected goals in specific areas.

You have so much to gain from developing these kinds of relationships. Seek out people God has put into your life that can be mentors and coaches. Ask questions and listen well. Show gratitude and be teachable. These relationships will be valuable gifts from God for years to come.

Father, bring to my mind the right people in my life who I can approach to be a mentor or coach. I do not know it all. I can use help navigating the world. Thank you that your Word offers solid counsel also. Help me take instruction with a right attitude.

NOT ONE FORGOTTEN

"Are not five sparrows sold for two pennies? Yet not one of them is forgotten in God's sight. But even the hairs of your head are all counted. Do not be afraid; you are of more value than many sparrows."

LUKE 12:6-7 NRSV

In a world of over seven billion people, it's easy to feel like just one insignificant face in the crowd. We wonder if God really cares about our lives and our thoughts and our heartbreaks. How could he with so many people to keep track of?

But if even the sparrow—who is such a small and seemingly insignificant animal—isn't forgotten or overlooked by God, how much more likely is he to know you and your heart? You are a human being, created in the image of God with a soul, mind, and will that are known by him. He's not far removed. He's not high above, looking down at you from a distance. He is with you. He knows the thoughts and the dreams of your heart even better than you do. Trust that his love for you is as intimate as it is vast.

Thank you, God, for including this verse in the Bible. You knew that in my insecurity, I might wonder if I mattered much to you. You took the time to reassure me that I do.

ALL GOD HAS

"Things which eye has not seen and ear has not heard,
And which have not entered the heart of man,
All that God has prepared for those who love Him."

1 CORINTHIANS 2:9 NASB

What God has for us is so much better than what we could dream up for ourselves. We think we know what's best for us. We think we know what would make us happy. If a certain someone loved us back, then we'd be happy. If we had success, fame, money, then we'd be happy.

The reality is that God created you—mind, body, and soul. He knows the inner workings of your heart, and he knows how to bring you true joy that won't ever fade. What he has in store for you will blow your mind. Don't spend your life desiring what you'll never have. Love God, invest in your relationship with him, and trust him to make you happy. The rewards that he will give are better than any reward the world could offer.

God, help me to trust that you desire for me to be happy. I don't want to look at your gifts as second best, because I know they aren't. You created me—I don't have to be afraid that you won't give what's best for me.

GIVE ME YOUR HEART

Give me your heart.
May your eyes take delight in following my ways.
PROVERBS 23:26 NLT

Our hearts are easily persuaded. We might be so sure of something in our heads, but if our hearts leads us elsewhere, we're almost left defenseless. It's hard to know how to trust our hearts. You're told constantly to follow your heart, but that can be hard when it pulls you in different directions.

That's why God says to give him your heart. He created that heart of yours, and he loves you. He doesn't want to see you heartbroken or disappointed. He wants to see you happy—living your best possible life. Following your heart alone can lead you places that you never wanted to go. But when you give your heart to God and then you follow him, you can trust that your happiness is in the best of hands.

Lord, I give you my heart. Take it and lead me wherever you want me to go. I don't want to spend these years of my life being heartbroken. I want to let you lead me to happiness because I know that the joy you give is everlasting.

ENEMIES AT PEACE

When people's lives please the Lord,
even their enemies are at peace with them.

PROVERBS 16:7 NLT

When you live in a way that's pleasing to God, it means you're leading a life marked by love, forgiveness, grace, and kindness. When people see you living that way, they can't find a bad thing to say about you. You've shown so much grace and love to others, what can they say against you? Even people that you've been at odds with in the past will feel their anger neutralized by your love.

Do your best to live according to the Word of God. Be someone who shares Christ's love just by the way you live. Maybe in the past you've had enemies. You've had people who didn't like you and didn't treat you well. But if you start to treat them in a way that is godly, their anger won't be able to stand. Conduct yourself with kindness. Act in patience. Offer mercy. Love above all else.

Thank you, God, that you've given me a way to live at peace with even my enemies. I want to lead a life that pleases you. Thank you for giving me all the tools to do that.

WEIGHT OF CRITICISM

Do not let anyone treat you as if you are unimportant because you are young. Instead, be an example to the believers with your words, your actions, your love, your faith, and your pure life.

1 TIMOTHY 4:12 NCV

Words can go a long way in your mind. They can either build you up, or they can crush your spirit. When you face a lot of negativity about anything, it's easy to want to give up. You don't feel strong enough to stand under the weight of criticism. Proving yourself sounds appealing, but far too difficult.

When Paul wrote these words to Timothy, he knew that Timothy would've faced some criticism for his age. Timothy was a pretty young guy who was put in a place of authority. Naturally, some people might have felt threatened by that. When people feel challenged or threatened, they can speak out in criticism.

If you're put in a position like Timothy was—where you're being criticized for something God told you to do—then extend grace to those in opposition. But continue doing the Lord's will. It will be worth it when you press through.

Lord, help me to focus on what you say about me over what others do.

SAFER IN HIS HANDS

When I am afraid, I will put my trust in You.
In God, whose word I praise,
In God I have put my trust; I shall not be afraid.
What can mere man do to me?

PSALM 56:3-4 NASB

Trust isn't easy. Trust means letting go. It means giving up control. Trust means believing that someone else can handle something as well or better than we can. Trust isn't usually our first reaction. Typically we want to hold on to the things that are valuable to us as tightly as we can—letting go of them is the last thing we want.

There is one person we can trust with everything we have. One person who can always handle it better than we can. God is trustworthy. He's never shown himself to be anything less. You can trust him with whatever situation comes your way. And you can trust him with your whole life. When fear overtakes you and you want to take back control, remember that your life is far safer in his hands than it would ever be in yours.

Lord, I know that you are trustworthy. When it comes to actually placing my life in your hands, I get fearful. Give me peace and the knowledge that you are to be trusted completely. You've never let me down, and I know that you never will.

ATTITUDE AND GRATITUDE

By Him let us continually offer the sacrifice of praise to God, that is, the fruit of our lips, giving thanks to His name.

HEBREWS 13:15 NKJV

Things are turning out differently than you expected. You got a diploma but no job, or not the job you thought you were preparing for all those years in school. You are living alone or with your parents or with ill-matched roommates. You have no inspiring hobbies and no money to travel the world. Bills and school debt are depressing and limiting your dreams.

What is the point of all this so-called adult life? One of the best ways to beat the blues is to focus on what you are thankful for, i.e. the age-old *count your blessings* advice. When you make a list of the many things that are good and helpful in your present life, you can more easily deal with the less desirable things. You become aware again how God has provided in the past, and gather courage to believe he will remain faithful today and tomorrow.

You may not be able to change your present situation, but you have total control over your attitude. Take a walk, select a favorite song, turn your thoughts to the goodness of God, and ask him to lift your cloud. Behind the darkness the sun is still shining.

Dear God, I am discouraged and struggling. Help me remember your faithfulness in the past, and help me to remember and believe that you haven't forgotten me. I have many blessings in my life. Thank you. Lift my head and help me change my attitude.

MOVING FROM SELF-FOCUS TO THINKING OF OTHERS

"If you love those who love you, what reward do you have? Do not even the tax collectors do the same?"

MATTHEW 5:46 ESV

A trend for the past decades directed parents, family members, teachers, athletic coaches, and the media to recognize each child's unique gifting and potential. Not a bad idea in theory. But, when a person grows up believing he is *special*, how does he consider the worth of others?

The definition of *special* suggests being better, more important, beyond usual, or above normal. Can *everyone* share that same description and still be *special*?

God considers us valuable and precious in his sight. Sending Jesus to pay for our sins demonstrated great love for us. We did nothing to merit this provision of salvation. With the assurance of his love, we are to love others, including those who may not love us back. We must move past our perceived entitlement and put the needs of others in our view.

To truly understand our talents, we must join the world's diverse community and discover what we have to offer. Finding significance outside ourselves is rewarding and *special*.

Dear God, help me to see my worth in you and my value in relationship to my fellow man. Give me a heart to serve and take my place in this world, not just take for myself. Let me love even unlovable people because you loved me first.

YOUR STORY

"Return to your home, and declare how much God has done for you." So he went away, proclaiming throughout the city how much Jesus had done for him.

LUKE 8:39 NRSV

No experience in your life is wasted. God always has something he can teach you. You may not even understand until years later why God brought you through something specific. But someday, it will all make sense.

Sometimes God will teach you things for your own growth. Other times it's not about you at all. Sometimes God will lead you through experiences or show you things so that you can impact someone's life with your story. Don't ever think that your story isn't good enough or interesting enough or happy enough or dramatic enough. Your story is your story—no one else has one just the same—and it will help someone in a way that nothing else could. Share your life story with others, encouraging them as you are able.

Heavenly Father, sometimes I don't understand why certain things happen to me. I don't know why my life looks the way that it does. But I trust that you have a unique plan for my life that couldn't be lived out by anyone else. Help me trust in your purposes.

BLESSED

You honor me by anointing my head with oil.
My cup overflows with blessings.

PSALM 23:5 NLT

One friend posts a photo of herself surrounded by more Christmas gifts than she can possibly appreciate; another shares an image of herself holding her new baby brother. Both are captioned the same: #blessed. But they're definitely *not* the same. So what constitutes a blessing?

God's blessings are far more likely to come in the form of intangibles than brightly wrapped boxes. The Lord's riches consist of things like patience, mercy, grace, peace, and kindness. Jesus gives us truth, freedom, and light. The Holy Spirit brings love, joy, and kindness. Gifts are great, but blessings are divine.

Father God, help me this Christmas season to remember the difference between gifts and blessings, and guide my heart toward blessings. Fill me with your kindness, generosity and grace. Allow me to be a blessing to everyone I meet.

WORTH WORRYING?

"Can all your worries add a single moment to your life?"
MATTHEW 6:27 NLT

It's easy to worry about the future. How am I going to do on my test? Are we going to win that big game? What will she say when I confront her? Will I get that job? These are a few examples that can send our minds racing.

What is the point of worry? Has worry ever helped anyone feel better? Has it ever solved the problem? No. Everything that you walk through with God is not going to be easy, but worry does not have to be part of it. If you seek God during difficult times, you can have confidence that he has heard you, and he will work out his good and perfect will.

God, I ask you to take care of my concerns. Help me to let them go. I know I will not always get what I want, and I can't always make everyone happy. Let my focus be on pleasing you.

COMPLETE HEALING

He heals the wounds of every shattered heart.
PSALM 147:3 TPT

When we look closely at ourselves, sometimes all we see is a broken and shattered remnant of what we once were. Sin, tragedy, rejection, or heartbreak can leave us feeling terrible. We wonder how we can pick up the pieces and be made whole again. In our brokenness, it's easy to feel hopeless. We try different methods to fill the void. We may look to relationships, things, or drugs to fix us. They can make us feel better temporarily, but eventually we realize that despite all our efforts, we still feel broken and incomplete.

Who could possibly love and care for such a broken and tattered person? Jesus. He loves you. *All of you.* God is faithful. He doesn't leave you alone in your brokenness; instead, he meets you in that place, takes your broken pieces, and tenderly puts you back together again. Why? Because he loves you too much to leave you in the state you are in.

Father, help me find wholeness in you. You are the only cure for my pain. The best doctors and medicines can't provide what you do. Your love is so deep it can even remove my scars.

DECEMBER

Oh, the depth of the riches both of the

wisdom and knowledge of God!

How unsearchable are His judgments

and unfathomable His ways!

ROMANS 11:33 NASB

SHOES AND RIGHTEOUSNESS

"For where your treasure is, there your heart will be also."
MATTHEW 6:21 NIV

Clothing, shoes, popularity, and name brands are some pretty common things valued by teenagers. It's pretty difficult not to value these things yourself. But what has *true* value? God wants us to focus on valuing things that are of him—things like love, generosity, righteousness, and honesty. These things bring lasting value because they add to the kingdom of heaven. Clothing and popularity are temporary; they can be taken away or destroyed in a single day.

If you happen to be popular, or can afford those name-brand boots, that's fine, but the moment you find yourself being motivated by, and becoming focused on, those things, you have given them too much value. You can't place equal value on shoes and righteousness; it just doesn't work that way.

God, remind me that you are not impressed by name brands. You are impressed by the love you see in my heart, the honest words I speak, and the generosity I display. Help my heart to be focused on those things so that they are what I pursue.

WALKING IN TRUTH

Lead me by your truth and teach me,
for you are the God who saves me.
All day long I put my hope in you.

Psalm 25:5 nlt

When we think of truth, we often think of confessing something we've done that was not wise. But truth is also shown in the encouraging words we say to others and the life we live as representatives of God. Living a life for truth means to live in a way that stands for truth in all circumstances. It can be difficult to speak truth when there is a chance we may offend someone, be met with awkward silence, or stand with the minority.

You may find yourself in a situation where you feel the need to stand for what is right, but you're unsure you can find the courage to do so. Likely the Holy Spirit is nudging you to speak out in truth. If you listen to that nudge and obey it, you open a door for God to touch others. God loves when you stand for him, especially during difficult times. He sees what you do and say during those times, and it blesses him beyond measure to see your boldness for him.

God, as I continue to walk in truth, will you use me in great ways? I know you are preparing a beautiful place for me in heaven!

DESERT SEASONS

Trust the Lord with all your heart,
and don't depend on your own understanding.
Remember the Lord in all you do,
and he will give you success.

PROVERBS 3:5-6 NCV

There can be seasons where things don't seem to work out in your favor and life seems harder than normal. It could be issues related to relationships, school, sports, or even family dynamics. When things are tough in these areas, it tends to greatly affect our feelings, our mindset, and even our trust in God. We might feel like we're in the desert all alone.

The good news is that God knows just where we are. We are not lost. Many times when we are walking through difficult situations, the Lord has allowed us to experience those difficulties to test what is in our hearts. He is refining and maturing us. Though it may feel like he is far away, he's actually close by, molding and shaping us like a potter does with clay.

God, when I experience seasons of difficulty, I want to keep trusting you. Help me to be teachable so I can see what you want me to learn. Thank you that there is a purpose for my seasons in the desert. They allow me an opportunity to grow closer to you.

TOMORROW'S TROUBLES

"Do not worry about tomorrow, for tomorrow will worry about its own things. Sufficient for the day is its own trouble."

MATTHEW 6:34 NKJV

Many young people are overwhelmed and overbooked. Life is fast and it doesn't want to slow down for anyone. There are multiple assignments to complete, tests to study for, instruments and sports to practice, chores to do, and friends you need to keep up with. And if that's not enough, you may feel it all needs to be done with excellence.

Time out! When you are feeling stress creep into your life, it is important to get back to where God wants you to be. He wants you right next to him. He wants to gently walk with you and teach you how to look at stressors differently. All you can do is try your best and that is enough. Did you get that? Trying your best is enough. Nobody expects you to have super powers.

God, I want to spend more time with you so I can begin to see things through your eyes. When I do, I know it will be easier to accept that trying my best is enough. Help me to do just that in the coming year—try my best!

GET SMART AND GO FISHING

How much better to get wisdom than gold,
to get insight rather than silver!

PROVERBS 16:16 NIV

The secret agent character in the late 1960's comedy series *Get Smart* seemed anything but smart. He made many mistakes and bumbled his agency training. Somehow he ended each episode as the unwise, yet resourceful and lucky, hero. Only in the movies, right?

What does *smart* look like? Getting fish from others or learning how to fish? Studying how to live wisely, which includes the making and handling of money, or depending on others to give you money?

At this point in your life, you need to learn so many things about work, relationships, time management, healthy living, and financial principles. Focus on learning and getting smart, and do not just focus on making money. Forget about winning the lottery or evading taxes. Read God's Word and other sources of proven information. Ask questions and listen to people who model wise living and demonstrate quality character. The investment to get wisdom will pay off at the right time.

Dear God, you are the source of all wisdom and wealth. Help me trust in your timing for financial provisions. For now, help me to spend my time learning to live well.

WISDOM AT EVERY TURN

If you are wise and understand God's ways, prove it by living an honorable life, doing good works with the humility that comes from wisdom.

JAMES 3:13 NLT

When you think of a wise person, is there anyone specific who comes to mind? What is it about that person that makes you think they are so wise? Certain qualities define a wise person. How they live their lives and *show* wisdom is the most important quality of all. It's more than talk; it's their walk. Boasting about their greatness or knowledge doesn't do it. Twisting situations to put themselves in a better light certainly doesn't either.

But living a life that follows the example Christ set is a great way to become wise. When we are humble, ask for others' opinions, seek knowledge, and live to serve, we find wisdom for ourselves. Be wise and follow the Lord!

Father, thank you for being the ultimate giver of wisdom. I want to seek your wisdom at every turn. I pray that I'd resist the temptation to tell people how knowledgeable I am. I pray I'd remain your humble servant.

ALREADY SELECTED

You are a chosen generation, a royal priesthood, a holy nation, His own special people, that you may proclaim the praises of Him who called you out of darkness into His marvelous light.

1 PETER 2:9 NKJV

Remember in school when you divide into groups, and slowly the captains select people for their team? For someone who isn't picked early on, the waiting can seem like forever. No one wants to be the last one picked. Guess what? God has already chosen you for his team. He picked you, right away, with no hesitation. He even calls you his special possession!

The rules of the game are simple: believe in him, follow his Word, speak out for him, do his work, and share his love with others. Tell everyone you know about the ways he has changed you for the better. He wants as many people as possible on his team, and he's calling you to add those members.

Lord, I praise you for all you've done for me. I pray I'd have the courage to be an active team member for your kingdom, sharing your love.

INDWELLING

A person who does not have the Spirit does not accept the truths that come from the Spirit of God. That person thinks they are foolish and cannot understand them, because they can only be judged to be true by the Spirit.

1 CORINTHIANS 2:14 NCV

If you met someone on the street and they said, "There's this guy that wants to live inside you and change your life," you'd probably run in the opposite direction. At the very least, it sounds a little goofy, doesn't it? And yet, it's true. There is someone who wants to take up residence within you! The person will give you the greatest joy you've ever known.

The Lord has given those who believe in him an incredible gift—his Holy Spirit. He's the one who resides with us and within us. He gives us the wisdom, knowledge, and power we wouldn't otherwise have without him. We can turn to him at any time.

Lord, I praise you today for the gift of your Holy Spirit. I know that without this gift, my life just wouldn't be the same. I'm thankful for it!

FACING THE SUN

If we say that we have fellowship with Him and yet walk in the darkness, we lie and do not practice the truth; but if we walk in the Light as He Himself is in the Light, we have fellowship with one another, and the blood of Jesus His Son cleanses us from all sin.

1 JOHN 1:6-7 NASB

When we accept Christ as our Savior, our world suddenly brightens. It's as if things that were in shadows have quickly come into the sun. Walking in that light takes continued effort. It means making a daily commitment to follow the example Christ has set for us—doing what's right and rejecting what's wrong. Choosing to make the same decisions we made before our life with God means we are choosing darkness. Choosing to make decisions according to his Word means we are choosing life.

Doesn't it feel great when the sun shines on your face? Use that as a reminder to turn your face to the one who is light. Walk with God each day of your life, staying close to him. If you choose him, you choose life.

Lord, thank you for shining your light upon me. Help me turn away from the darkness in my life.

WORRY-FREE

Do not fear, for I am with you;
do not be dismayed, for I am your God.
I will strengthen you and help you;
I will uphold you with my righteous right hand.

ISAIAH 41:10 NIV

God promises to strengthen you and to help you with whatever you are going through right now. Stress, fear, and feeling overwhelmed are no match for the Lord. He's going to hold you steady when you feel too wobbly to stand on your own.

God is with you. He is your God, and he is good. He never intended for you to live weighed down with worry. Instead, he'd love for you to throw all your cares on him. God is strong enough to take care of them. He's big enough to handle whatever you're willing to give him. You just have to allow him to help you.

Lord, thank you for strengthening me. I know that I do not have to fear because you are there for me.

ULTIMATE GPS

My eyes are ever on the Lord,
for only he will release my feet from the snare.

PSALM 25:15

It's common sense to watch where you're going or you'll get tripped up. When it comes to walking with God, though, it's a different story. Instead of looking ahead and watching your every move, the Bible says to look directly at the Lord, every moment of your life. He'll keep you from whatever traps you may fall into.

Spend less time looking at the details of your life and more time with your eyes fixed on God. He is the ultimate GPS, and he will lead you exactly where you need to go. It's only when you take your eyes off him, that you'll fall right smack into the trap that the enemy sets for you. Stay close to God for direction.

Lord, thank you for directing me where to go and what steps to take. I pray that my eyes will always be on you.

BLESSING OF FRIENDS

Two people are better off than one, for they can help each other succeed. If one person falls, the other can reach out and help. But someone who falls alone is in real trouble.

ECCLESIASTES 4:9-10 NLT

Friends are one of God's greatest gifts. They bring joy, encouragement, and companionship. Good friends bring out the best in us and always point us toward Christ. True friends aren't afraid to get messy with us. They know us at our best, but also at our worst. They aren't put off by authenticity but instead prefer it over a surface-level relationship.

God never intended for us to be alone. He created this need in us to need each other and to love each other deeply. God gave us friends so we can help each other through life's tough times, knowing that there are plenty of times when two people are better than one. If you are lonely and need a friend, ask God to bring one into your life.

Lord, thank you for the blessing of wonderful friends. Thank you for giving me friends to laugh with, cry with, and pray with. Teach me how to love and serve my friends well.

FAITH AND FEAR

"You of little faith, why are you so afraid?"
Then he got up and rebuked the winds and the waves,
and it was completely calm.

MATTHEW 8:26 NIV

Fear takes many shapes—some are afraid to make bold decisions, afraid to travel, or afraid of being alone. You can fear death, sickness, or even poverty. Whatever you fear can keep you from finding deep joy and freedom in life. It can have the power to influence what you do or don't do and the power to silence your heart if you allow it to.

Jesus and his disciples were in the middle of a fierce storm when the disciples started to freak out. "Lord, save us!" they said. "We're going to drown!"

"Where's your faith?" Jesus asked. Then he simply calmed the wind and sea.

You see, faith is the opposite of fear. Fear says, "I don't believe God is able to take care of me." Faith says, "God is powerful and loving and always in control." Believing in God gives you courage because you realize God is who he says he is and he will do what he promised—he will be with you always.

Jesus, give me a heart filled with faith in your love and your power. As I keep believing in you, grow my courage. Thank you that you never leave me.

LOVE YOUR ENEMIES

"You have heard that it was said, 'Love your neighbor and hate your enemy.' But I tell you, love your enemies and pray for those who persecute you."

MATTHEW 5:43-44 NIV

Love your enemies? Pray for them? Really? How? Sometimes we feel justified to hate someone or be angry. But God says we *must* love others. While this may seem impossible, Jesus gave us our greatest example of love. Even when he was being beaten, persecuted, and hated, he begged God to have mercy on his killers. His love allowed him to see deeper than their actions. He saw beyond their anger and looked directly into their hearts. His love for them moved him to compassion and grace.

To choose to love someone who is against us and who has harmed us is one of the hardest commandments. It requires humility to put our anger and hate aside, get down on our knees, and *pray for* our enemies. Hard? Yes. But it's not impossible. Not with God.

Lord, I want to love my enemies the way you love them. Move me to compassion and take away my pride. May my love for you lead me to love those around me deeply, even those that hurt me.

GUILTY OR NOT

As high as the heavens are above the earth,
so great is his love for those who fear him;
as far as the east is from the west,
so far has he removed our transgressions from us.

PSALM 103:11-12 NIV

How high are the heavens above the earth? How far is the east from the west? If you can measure that, you'll be able to measure the scope of God's love and forgiveness—infinitesimal! That's how far God removes our sins from us.

As believers, guilt has no place in our lives. Yet it ever so quietly attempts to make our lives its home. It stops us from moving past sin and into the arms of Jesus. It keeps us from stepping into complete healing and restoration. Focusing on regret actually stops us from living in grace. God doesn't want us to be weighed down with guilt or wrapped up in self-condemnation. If you are battling guilt—stop! It is not worth your time and energy. Instead believe in the bigness and greatness of God who freely forgives you.

When I make a mistake, God, guilt seems to pull me down. Thank you that when you wash away my sins, you also free me from guilt and condemnation.

BEAUTIFUL HUMILITY

Humble yourselves before the Lord, and he will lift you up.

JAMES 4:10 NIV

Humbling ourselves and admitting we're wrong or have made a mistake can be a hard pill to swallow. Acknowledging our weaknesses and exposing ourselves to judgment and scrutiny can be even harder. Pride keeps us distant from God and others. When we are proud, we rob people of the chance to love us despite our brokenness, despite our mistakes. Pride makes us hard and unchangeable. If we are proud, we leave no room for growth.

Humility, though, can be such a beautiful thing. Humility restores broken relationships and brings us closer to God. The more humble we are, the more we are made aware of God's grace, mercy, and love in our lives. Humbling ourselves gives us the chance to change for the better.

God, it's never easy for me to admit I'm wrong. I need your grace and mercy to change me. Replace my pride with meekness. May I always be aware of how desperately I need you. I'd rather run confidently into your arms than wallow in my pride.

BEFORE YOU SPEAK

*Those who are careful about what they say
keep themselves out of trouble.*

PROVERBS 21:23 NCV

Shoot off a quick text. Post a quick tweet. Make a casual comment. It's easy to do any of these without giving much thought to what we're putting out there. Many times, we do it out of a reaction to what someone else said. We're mostly concerned with painting ourselves in the best possible light. We forget, though, that everything we say has an effect on the ones who hear or see it. That impact can be positive, but it can also be negative.

Before you communicate, do you consider how it will affect people? Next time, take a minute first. Consider the potential impact of your words and ask, "Is what I'm about to do going to be beneficial or potentially harmful?"

Lord, help me think before I speak. I don't want to mindlessly put my words out there; I want them to have purpose. I can impact people with what I say, and I don't want to abuse that power. Give me wisdom and restraint when I speak.

WORTH ALL YOUR LOVE

Yet I hold this against you:
You have forsaken the love you had at first.

REVELATION 2:4 NIV

When you first come to God, you give him all of your heart. Your love is whole, passionate, and honest. As time goes on, other loves become tempting to you. You begin to divide your devotion to God by looking to others, and it hinders your relationship with him.

Always keep yourself going back to the love you had for God at first. Remind yourself what it felt like when your heart first said yes to him. Nothing and no one in this world is worth loving the way that he is. No one else will love you in return with as much passion, grace, and constant love. No one else is worth all of your love.

God, I remember what it felt like when I first said yes to following you. My love was sincere, complete, and pure. Since then I've gotten distracted by other things that so easily pull me away. Help me to keep my heart completely focused on you.

KNOW YOUR HEART

You have searched me, Lord,
and you know me.

PSALM 139:1 NIV

High school is the one time when you can completely devote yourself to finding out who you really are in Christ. You're old enough to know how to seek the Lord and his presence on your own. At the same time, you're young enough to be free from the demands of adulthood, marriage, and parenting.

Use this time to explore who you are, what you like, what you're good at, and the gifts that God has placed in you. Take advantage of this time to discover the extent of your heart. As a result, when you are ready to give your heart and love away to another person, you will be able to say with confidence that you know exactly what you are giving. Know your own heart—and come to know it through the God who created it.

Lord, help me discover more of who you've created me to be. Help me to give my love away when it is the right time—after I have come to know my heart and all that you created me to be.

FOREVER LOVE

Give thanks to the LORD, for he is good,
for his steadfast love endures forever.

PSALM 136:1 ESV

We see a lot of love that doesn't last long. People get together, claim to be in love, and then want nothing to do with each other a few months or years later.

There is one love that is promised to us for eternity. One love that will never change, never lessen, and never be removed. God promises us his love forever—and God never breaks his promises. He loves you for always. Not just for days when you look pretty. Not just for moments when you're good. Not just for the times you obey him and please him. For always. No conditions. No exceptions. Just pure, complete, eternal love.

Thank you, Jesus, for loving me unconditionally. Thank you that in a world of less than perfect love, yours is perfect. I want to love you more each day. Cause my heart to respond to your love and to feel it.

A LIVING SACRIFICE

Therefore, I urge you, brothers and sisters, in view of God's mercy, to offer your bodies as a living sacrifice, holy and pleasing to God—this is your true and proper worship.

ROMANS 12:1 NIV

Sacrifice. It's not a very comfortable word is it? What does it mean to be a living sacrifice? As God's followers and children, we should live in a way that honors and blesses him. It is so difficult to live that kind of life with all of the temptations of this world and everything at our fingertips. In fact, we can't live a holy and pleasing life *and* give into temptation. We fall into the trap of doing what we want: buying too much stuff, dressing to fit in, gossiping about others, being ungrateful— and these are just a few things we need to watch out for.

If you practice each week to work on an area in your life that you feel hasn't blessed the Lord, then you will feel something change, and you'll receive the confidence that only your Heavenly Father can give. By living this way, you are sacrificing your desires and truly worshiping him. *That* is pleasing to God.

God, help me to sacrifice the things that I want in order to serve you and live the way you want me to live. I know it is better for me to live your way, so help me continue to choose that.

LET HIM IN

"Look! I stand at the door and knock. If you hear my voice and open the door, I will come in, and we will share a meal together as friends."

REVELATION 3:20 NLT

You know what is interesting about this verse? It's that you have to open the door. Jesus will knock. He might knock many times. But he won't come in until you've opened the door for him. Jesus won't force his way into your heart or your life because he wants to be welcomed in.

Jesus won't make you love him. He won't force you to follow him. He gives you full freedom to choose. Even once that door has been opened, closeness with the Lord means seeking him every day. It means reading his Word, listening to his voice, and letting him hear yours. It means allowing him to have full say in your life. It means sharing your heart with him. He will come knocking because he wants a relationship with you. But you must make a choice to invite him in.

Lord, I've heard you knocking. I've been afraid to let you in because, although I know there's a reward, I know there's a cost too. But I want to invite you in. Come into my heart, Jesus. Come and be Lord of my life.

THE NAME OF THE LORD

By Him let us continually offer the sacrifice of praise to God, that is, the fruit of our lips, giving thanks to His name.

HEBREWS 13:15 NKJV

Jesus, King of kings and Lord of lords, came to earth to live as a man, suffered cruelty, gave his life by dying on a cross, all to know you. It's sad when people devalue Christ's name by using it as a swear word. When someone takes the name of the Lord in vain, they are flippantly using a name that is above all other names.

God created your mouth and fashioned your lips to be able to speak, to sing, to praise. The same mouth that he so carefully created should be speaking his name only in thanks, in praise, in wonder. When you open your mouth to speak the name of the Lord, check yourself first. Ask yourself if the way you are speaking about him brings him honor or if it disrespects him and disregards what he's done.

Lord, forgive me for the times I've used your name carelessly. Help me speak your name only with utmost respect and the highest honor.

THIS IS POSSIBLE

Jesus looked at them and said, "With man this is impossible, but with God all things are possible."

MATTHEW 19:26 NIV

Do you believe that God is able to do the impossible? We read our Bibles that Jesus did all sorts of crazy things that we can't even imagine seeing today—healing a blind man, raising a man from the dead, transforming five loaves and two fish into food for thousands. We talk all the time about how great and powerful God is, but have we seen it for ourselves?

God's power hasn't lessened, no matter how long ago those miracles happened. He is an unchanging God who is always constant. He is still doing miracles all around us—maybe we just aren't looking for them. In our age of technology and advancements, we tend to explain away almost anything with science and calculated theory. We lose our faith in exchange for rationale, and somewhere in there we've lost our miracles too. Look around you today for the miracles God is working everywhere. They are happening—you just have to have faith enough to see them.

I know, God, that you are just as powerful today as you were when Jesus walked the earth. You are capable of anything because there is no one above you. Help me to trust you for miracles and to have faith when you move.

JOURNEY OF HOPE

"Look, the virgin shall conceive and bear a son,
and they shall name him Emmanuel,
which means, 'God is with us.'"

MATTHEW 1:23 NRSV

The day had almost arrived! There were many people waiting for the birth of Jesus. The Jews had long awaited their Messiah, Mary and Joseph were waiting for their firstborn baby, and the Wise Men were looking for the sign. Jesus was the hope that they all looked toward.

There is always a journey involved in waiting for great expectations to be fulfilled. The Jews were preparing themselves for the appointed time, Mary and Joseph had to travel to another town, and the Wise Men had to follow the star. In our own lives, we sometimes forget that the journey is part of the fulfilment of the things that we hope for.

Are you waiting and hoping for something great to be fulfilled? Take a moment today to reflect on the journey of those that waited expectantly for their Savior.

God, I pray that hope will remain in my heart
for what is to come.

OUR FIGHT

*Our fight is not against people on earth but against
the rulers and authorities and the powers of this world's
darkness, against the spiritual powers of evil in the
heavenly world.*

EPHESIANS 6:12 NCV

It's easy to think that what we can't see doesn't exist. The concept of angels and demons can sound eerie and almost fantastical to us. In our minds, we have cartoon characters or media images connected with those beings, and to a point, it removes their reality. There *is* a spiritual realm that truly exists; it's real and it's not to be messed with.

There is a war going on in the heavenly realm. Be careful how you engage in this battle. Be aware of what you let into your mind and heart. Remember also that God is more powerful than any other being in this universe. You don't have to fear the powers of darkness, but you must be aware. Call on the name of Jesus and claim his power over your life. He is more than able to keep you safe and to fight your battles.

God, I admit that I don't think often enough about the spiritual battle going on. Thank you for your power on my life. I know that I don't have to fear the darkness. Help me to stay alert. Don't let me be pulled in by things that aren't of you.

YOU LOVED THEM

It wasn't their swords that took the land.
It wasn't their power that gave them victory.
But it was your great power and strength.
You were with them because you loved them.

PSALM 44:3 NCV

Do you ever feel powerless? Like you're trapped in your own life, unable to fix what's broken? You know you can't save yourself; you just aren't armed for it. Life can be hard. There are so many things that will come at you from a million directions and make you feel defenseless. Drama with friends, trouble with parents, mistakes you've made that you don't know how to fix.

Don't lose heart. You are not left alone to fight your battles. You have a God who loves you enough to fight for you. He is powerful and strong. And he is compelled by his love for you. Beloved, he died for you. What makes you think he wouldn't be willing to put himself into your fight and win it for you? You are his child, and he loves you.

Thank you, God, that you are here to fight my battles. I need your strength in my life. I feel powerless to save myself and know I'll never be able to. You are with me because you love me, and that makes all the difference.

TENDER LOVE

"I am a God who is near," says the LORD.
"I am also a God who is far away.
No one can hide where I cannot see him," says the LORD.
"I fill all of heaven and earth," says the LORD.

JEREMIAH 23:23-24 NCV

God is so loving and tender toward us that sometimes we forget just how majestic and powerful he is. Yes, he's the God who keeps our tears in a bottle. Yes, he's the God who bends low to listen to us cry. But he's also the God who separated night from day. He's the God who sent a flood that destroyed the entire earth. He's the God who is more powerful than any devil.

As we are comforted by God's tenderness, let's not forget his greatness. His power is what makes his tenderness all the more sweet. Is there anything more precious than seeing a big strong man cradling a new baby? Something about all that power holding all that fragility is a picture of tender love—of God's love.

You are the all-powerful God. You could snuff out my life in a second. Instead, you choose to love me. You choose to hold me. You choose to be patient with me. Thank you.

RUN AWAY

So run away from sexual sin. Every other sin people do is outside their bodies, but those who sin sexually sin against their own bodies.

1 CORINTHIANS 6:18 NCV

When we're young, it can be hard to realize how our sexual behavior will affect us later in life. Sadly, this is a lesson that's often learned the hard way. If you were to ask a lot of older Christian women about some of their biggest regrets in life, this is the topic that often comes up.

When sexual immorality comes into play, there really is only one thing to do. Flee. Run away. Get out of any relationship or any situation that causes you to fall. If you continue to sin sexually, you will regret it later in life. That's a guarantee. If you've already jumped this fence and you've sinned, then ask God to build an even bigger fence around your purity. He can restore what's been lost. Use his grace to move forward in purity from this point on.

Lord, help me to stay pure. Keep me out of situations that tempt me to do something I'll spend my life regretting.

TAKING UP SPACE

Cast all your anxiety on him, because he cares for you.
1 PETER 5:7 NRSV

You're wide awake, staring at the ceiling. You check the time…again. Adding to the worry of whatever's keeping you awake, you're now anxious about the fact you're not sleeping. *What if I sleep through my alarm? What if I never fall asleep at all?*

Whether an upcoming test, a text that never came, a sick relative, or general uneasiness, anxiety is a real problem. The author of the Bible knew this, which is why so there are so many Scriptures about it. Anxiety, worry, fear, stress…whatever you call it, the solution is the same—get rid of it! Picture the thing you dread in your hand. Now toss it to Jesus. He actually *wants* your problems. Your worries are taking up space in your heart, space he wants to fill with his joy.

Lord, I hold in my hands all that keeps me from being filled with your joy. Your Word tells me to cast it on you, so here it is. Thank you, Jesus, for caring enough to take it away.

TRUTHFUL AND KIND

The wicked flee when no one pursues,
but the righteous are as bold as a lion.

PROVERBS 28:1 NRSV

If someone were to pick up your phone and start reading your messages out loud in class, what would happen? Would you be at risk of hurting friends, getting in serious trouble, being completely humiliated, or just being a little embarrassed?

No one enjoys having their privacy invaded, although having conversations revealed present more of a problem for some than for others. Whether you can hold your head high or need to duck behind a notebook depends on how closely your private self reflects your public image. Are you as honest, kind, and sincere as people perceive you to be?

If the thought of someone going through your phone has your stomach in knots, perhaps it's time to ask yourself a few questions. Are your words both truthful and kind? Do your conversations build people up, or tear them down?

Jesus, I want to be the kind of person who could walk boldly into any room, even after all my secrets were revealed. Help me grow in kindness, truth, and love. Help me be more like you.